THE RESPONSIBLE CHURCH
AND
THE FOREIGN MISSION

PETER BEYERHAUS
and
HENRY LEFEVER

(Based on *Die Selbständigkeit der jungen Kirchen als missionarisches Problem* by
Peter Beyerhaus)

D1432323

WILLIAM B. EERDMANS PUBLISHING COMPANY
GRAND RAPIDS, MICHIGAN

First Published in America by
William B. Eerdmans Publishing Company, 1964
© World Dominion Press, 1964

MADE AND PRINTED IN GREAT BRITAIN BY
CHARLES BIRCHALL & SONS LTD.
LONDON AND LIVERPOOL

CONTENTS

v

PART TWO: THE PROBLEM IN THE HISTORY OF MISSIONS

PART THREE: THE THEOLOGICAL PROBLEM OF THE RESPONSIBLE CHURCH

CONTENTS

INTRODUCTION

'MISSIONS have always had problems, but now missions themselves have become a problem.' These words of the late Professor Freytag of Hamburg have been quoted many times recently and point to a very real bewilderment in the missionary world today. Sometimes we are tempted to look back nostalgically to the days when the only problems of missions were apparently those of balancing budgets and of finding enough recruits to take up the tasks which were waiting to be done, to the days when there was a clear-cut distinction between 'Christendom' and the 'heathen and other unenlightened nations'—as one great missionary society called them.

The problem of missions today arises, in part, from a new approach to the non-Christian religions of Asia and Africa. Recent discussions, like those at the meeting of the World Council of Churches at New Delhi, have raised again the question of revelation in these religions. Christians may have theological difficulties over this question, but they are not, for the most part, happy about dismissing the non-Christian faiths as mere idolatry and superstition. Some argue that we cannot rule out an element of divine revelation wherever men have honestly sought after God, but they are not sure what is the relation between that and the revelation of God in Jesus Christ. The much talked of resurgence of non-Christian religions forces this question upon us with peculiar relevance at the present time, but the question is there, inherent in the very nature of the Gospel. 'He who is not against me is with me,' said Jesus, and the writer of the fourth Gospel declared him to be 'the light which lighteth every man that cometh into the world'.

A hundred years ago, missionaries were so convinced, and so rightly convinced, of the uniqueness of God's act of revelation in Jesus Christ that they were not always able to recognize God acting apart from Christ. Today, some missionaries and their supporters are so bewildered by apparent signs of God's self-revelation in the religious experience of non-Christians, that they find it difficult to declare the uniqueness of His revelation in Christ. Non-Christians call the older approach of Christian missions 'spiritual imperialism'; many Christians feel the new approach to be nothing short of denial of the fundamentals of their faith.

But this is only one aspect of the problem of missions today. Apart altogether from the challenge of the non-Christian faiths, there is another challenge, from within the household of faith itself. Congregations in the West may continue to think of missionary work in terms of those of their own number who have gone overseas to proclaim the Gospel to the 'heathen', but the missionaries themselves know that the greater part of their time is given to work among the local Christians, directing their efforts to the building up of the Church. This has been an objective of foreign missions since the earliest days, and especially since the beginning of the modern missionary movement.

William Carey, more than 150 years ago, while yet with only a handful of converts, laid far-sighted plans for the organization of the Indian Church, with local pastors and evangelists working under the supervision of the foreign missionaries. He saw already that, as the Church grew, and as doors for the Gospel opened in the non-Christian world, the work would far exceed the powers of the missionaries themselves. Still earlier in the history of modern missions, other missionaries and mission-boards saw the development of an indigenous ministry, and finally of an autonomous Church, freed from the leading-strings of missionaries, as something more than a matter of pastoral or evangelistic expediency. It was not, they saw, just a question of the over-burdened Western missionary seeking the co-operation of local workers for the growing work of the Church. There was a theological necessity, too, which made it not only expedient, but right, to build up the Church, both in power and in responsibility.

The slogan : 'Let the Church be the Church' was not expressed, in so many words, for over a century, but the thought behind the words was there, almost from the beginning. If the Church is really to be the Church, and not just a dependency of a foreign mission, itself in most cases a voluntary society rather than a Church, it must be a responsible body, making its own decisions and, as far as lies within its powers, supporting its work with its own resources.

These thoughts lie behind the words of Henry Venn, who was Secretary of the Anglican Church Missionary Society from 1841 to 1871, that the 'euthanasia' of a mission takes place when the missionary is able to resign all pastoral work into the hands of the indigenous ministry and congregation. Nor was Henry Venn alone in these thoughts. Another mission board secretary, the American Congregationalist, Rufus Anderson, had already, in 1836, declared the policy of the American Board of Commissioners for Foreign Missions to be the creation of an indigenous ministry.

'Heathen nations must be rendered independent of Christendom for their religious teachers as soon as possible.'

Venn and Anderson were in frequent communication with one another and undoubtedly influenced each other's thinking. Together they came to formulate the missionary task, as far as the building of the Church was concerned, as that of 'preparing the new churches for self-government', and they saw this task to be closely related to that of encouraging the churches to achieve self-support. Anderson carried the task a stage further when, in his *Outline of Missionary Policy*, published in 1856, he declared the chief goal of missions to be the encouragement of the new churches in the task of self-propagation. From that time, the tri-partite aim of the missionary's church-work was declared by both these leaders to be the aiding of the Church in its efforts towards 'self-government, self-support and self-propagation'. If we today see something unbiblical in all this emphasis on self, particularly in relation to the government of the Church, and in the close connexion between self-government and self-support, we need to recognize the genuine desire of these early leaders to encourage new churches, composed, for the most part, of simple folk with 'not many wise, not many noble, not many mighty', in a true sense of Christian responsibility which is an essential character-istic of the Church.

The Church-problem of missions today is to see how the responsibility of the local Church is to be related to the equally deep sense of responsibility, especially for mission, still held by the churches from which the majority of missionaries come. Vagueness on this relation is one of the most significant factors in the sense of 'lost directness' of which Professor Freytag also spoke at the Ghana meeting of the International Missionary Council in 1959, a lost directness felt in the churches which have been among the most generous and devoted supporters of foreign missions, and also among the missionaries themselves. This lost directness is not to be dispersed by too facile an assertion that 'of course missionaries are still needed'. Missionaries frequently ask what they are needed for, and do not always get a convincing reply.

With the emphasis on the Church in current missionary thinking, it is difficult to see missionary work today as other than a form of 'inter-church aid'. This is, indeed, a very noble object, but it is not the aim of the missionaries and their societies as it has traditionally been presented to the supporting churches. That is one important reason for the present concern with 'missionary education'. In spite of regular missionary deputation work, and a continuous flow of supporting literature of an increasingly thoughtful quality, there is still something near to a revolution necessary in the missionary thinking of the churches.

Both older and younger churches need to understand missions as activities within the world mission of the Church. Within that world mission there is room for inter-church aid. A Church which feels that its own responsibility has been discharged when the new Church is established as a self-governing, and wholly or largely self-supporting body, has never rightly understood its missionary responsibility. 'If you want to go home when we have achieved a responsible existence of our own, you should never have come,' said the Asian Christian leader Dr. D. T. Niles not long ago. The motive for the original coming was a false one. Similarly, if the immediate reaction of a newly autonomous Church is to declare its self-sufficiency, its independence of any other Church, that reaction, though possibly understandable as a natural human reaction to paternalistic rule, is not a completely responsible reaction. It is a sign of immaturity, not of maturity.

The problem of missions today is, above everything, that of understanding these activities afresh in such a manner as to make clear that missions are particular expressions of the world mission of the Church. They may include a greater or less degree of inter-church aid, but the aim is 'mission', and the 'aid' an expression of the grace of the Lord Jesus Christ, which is the very heart of the Gospel the Church is sent to proclaim to the world.

Great efforts have been made in the course of the last generation, that is in the immediately recent past, to seek a solution of the problems raised by the developing autonomy of the churches which have arisen as a consequence of the work of foreign missions. It is not surprising that there should be such problems : they are the expression in the life of the Church of those perennial and universal tensions in the life of the family. A satisfying solution in each case, in Church and family, requires the grace of the Lord Jesus Christ and an understanding of personal relations in the light of the Holy Spirit. Nor is it surprising that the problems should appear in different forms in different situations, for, again, that is true of relations generally between different generations. But the continued existence of these problems in Church-Mission relations is a major source of frustration, and what Dr. Freytag calls 'lost directness', on both sides.

Much has been written of late on the subject of 'missionary paternalism', and no one with any experience of missionaries will pretend that they are not fallible mortals like other people, prone to the same temptations as other men, and, in particular, the temptation to self-importance. The pioneer missionary among simple folk is bound to feel responsible for them, and this very sense of responsibility can easily become perverted into a desire to impose his own will upon others, and to regard any opposing of this desire as a form of obstructionism. It would be a wicked slander, however, to assert that pioneer missionaries, in general, were filled with any such desire : that they were, as a class, Prosperos trying with no hope of success to make civilized and mature persons out of rude Calibans. Our present-day tendency to represent the pioneers in such a light may well be due to a necessity to come to terms with our own consciences over the question of our lack of the pioneers' sense of identification and responsibility. No one who lacks these fundamental missionary qualities has the right to talk of the paternalism of those who have—or had—them. In fact, as we have already seen from the example of Carey, some of the greatest of the early pioneers were most concerned for the growth of responsibility, and, indeed, autonomy in the new churches.

Henry Venn's vision of the self-supporting Church arising out of the work of missionaries was not something conjured up in his London headquarters. It was based on conversations with missionaries who, we may safely assume, were for the most part wholly in sympathy with his policy, if they did not actually suggest it to him. The very immensity of their task must have prompted some of these over-burdened missionaries to seek the co-operation of indigenous workers and to endeavour to build up a self-supporting, self-governing and self-propagating Church. This may be called, with considerable justification, the most characteristic missionary attitude of the 'Great Century' of foreign missions, which came to an end with the outbreak of the First World War. The emphasis on the need for a responsible Church has not been in any way weaker since that period, but it has been made from a different standpoint. Again, with the analogy of the family in mind, we can say that the father's hopes and ambitions for his young children are succeeded by the hopes and ambitions of the children themselves as they begin to find irksome the paternal restraints and directions of their infant life.

In the period after World War One, the rising tide of nationalism in Asia and Africa encouraged the churches there to adopt the old missionary formula, often (how like the adolescent!) under the impression that it was a formula of their own devising. This was the period of the greatest frustration, on both sides, and yet, we may believe, the burden many were called upon to bear was part of the labour of the Spirit in bringing forth a new creation, the ecumenical Church of the twentieth century.

In this present period the question is not the missionary one, how local Christians can be called to help in the work, nor the Church one, how mission-churches can become independent, but the ecumenical question: 'What is the nature of the Church's autonomy and how can this autonomy be reconciled with the unity and catholicity of the Church?' In this form, the problem is still unsolved and is causing more uncertainty and even distress than ever before.

There is uncertainty and distress in the newly autonomous churches of Africa and the East as their members sense a weakening of relations with churches overseas with whom their destinies have been intimately joined. There is an element of the 'have your cake and eat it' principle here, as when territories emerge from colonial to self-rule, but assume confidently that the former colonial power, while carefully refraining from any continued domination, will be ready at all times and for old times' sake to come to the aid of the new nation if asked to do so. Certainly, there will be a bond of affection in these circumstances, but the circumstances are different for both parties and the expression of the affection may well be in different terms, no less real than the former expression, but all the same different.

This difference is not always understood, particularly by simple folk who see only that where formerly they could rely, almost as a matter of course, on the ready response of the 'fathers' overseas to their children's requests, they cannot so confidently expect such a response any longer. 'Have the fathers forgotten us?' is a question actually heard today from the lips of African and Asian Christians. It is not only in the political sphere that some newly autonomous peoples are asking, rather sadly : 'Is this what independence means?'.

New attitudes are called for in the minds of members of new churches, as well as in the minds of the churches which, for many years, have been the chief supporters of missionary work. We have already noted how these supporters still too often think of the work in the terms of 'our missionaries'. The Church overseas remains an interesting concept, but lacks, for the majority of mission-supporters, the compelling emotional appeal of the old-fashioned picture of the pioneer missionary preaching in distant lands to simple folk who had never heard the Gospel before.

Uncertainty and distress are not merely to be found among naïve supporters, who ought to know better after so many years of missionary deputation and promotion work. They are to be found in the minds of some of the most enlightened missionaries and mission-boards. Autonomy has been given to the erstwhile dependent Church, but what of the continuing sense of responsibility to God for the proclamation of the Gospel, the continuing sense of vocation, not just in the Church in general, but in a particular Church or denomination, to proclaim the Gospel in countries overseas? How indirect can you get in this matter of

15

proclaiming the Gospel? Can you delegate your whole responsibility so that you never question what is being done—or not done—on the spot?

There is a very real sense of distress in the minds of many missionaries and their boards today : they continue to feel God's call to proclaim the Gospel, but also feel committed to a policy of church-autonomy which gives them no opportunity to do that work unless the local Church invites them to do so in its area. When, as is so often the case in both East and West, the local Church is inward-looking rather than outward-looking, the result for the man or Church with a call to mission can be a major spiritual dilemma.

Under these circumstances, the question is forced upon us, whichever side 'we' are on : have we properly understood the nature of the Church's autonomy? Is autonomy a theological concept anyway and, if it is not, how is our concept of autonomy—taken over into the Church's life very largely from philosophical or political realms of thought—to be checked, and, if necessary, changed by the experience of the Lordship of Christ and the unity and universality of the Church?

There is a steadily growing conviction among Christians, partly as a result of the deeper understanding of the Bible, and partly as a result of the ecumenical movement, that this word 'autonomy' cannot be used of the individual believer or his Church without qualification. The same is true of the classic concepts of modern missionary policy : self-government, self-support and self-propagation. For one thing, the New Testament speaks of 'self' only as something to be denied, or at least as something to be discovered only through being set aside and forgotten. The secular use of these expressions has no relation to the Christian life. It is as far away from the Bible as is the idea of a Church in bondage to foreign powers and cultures—or even to other churches.

The secular meaning of phrases such as 'self-government', 'self-support', and 'self-propagation' is altogether different from that understood by evangelicals like Henry Venn. He and others like him assumed they were dealing with the converted, both missionaries and local Christians. They assumed the rule of Christ before they spoke of self-rule. Without Christ's Lordship, there was no theological significance in either dependence or autonomy. The danger is that we should use these concepts without relation to the Lordship of Christ, a danger abundantly realized in the history of modern missions. We are not called to abandon them altogether. A Church is not mature, it has not grown up into the full stature of Christian humanity, and is, therefore, not really a Church at all, if it is not self-governing, self-supporting and self-propagating, but it is true for churches and for individuals that 'he who would seek to save his soul, or self, shall lose it'.

'If anyone wishes to be a follower of mine,' said Jesus, 'he must leave self behind, but if a man will let himself be lost for my sake he will find his true self' (Matthew 16.24f *NEB*). There is thus a 'sort of self' and a 'true self'. The 'sort of self' is important, but it is only a shadow of the 'true self'. It matters that a Church should be self-governing, but this 'autonomy' is not the most vital principle of its being : the vital thing is, we might say, Christonomy, the 'rule of Christ'. When Christ rules there is the true self, and where His Spirit is there is true liberty. True liberty demands the existence of autonomy in relation to others, but both we ourselves and the 'others' are under the rule of Christ. That is the only liberty, the only autonomy, which is worth talking about and that is the autonomy which we are concerned to define in our study of Church-Mission relations in the modern world.[1]

[1] Perhaps autonomy is an unsatisfactory word to use in this connexion; it has become debased in secular use. In the German book on which the present work is based, the word used was *Selbständigkeit*, literally 'independence'. No wonder the author sees this attribute of the younger churches as a missionary problem. The expression 'responsible selfhood' has been suggested as a better rendering of the original, but, while the *Oxford Concise Dictionary* admittedly gives the word 'selfhood', it also notes that this is 'rare'. The subject is complicated sufficiently without seeking to clarify it by the use of obscure and unidiomatic expressions. Perhaps the word 'responsible' by itself would be sufficient. But the 'responsible Church', though an important and challenging expression, is really too wide a term for the subject we are considering. Our subject is 'the responsible Church and the ecumenical relationship', again a rather cumbrous expression, but at least it avoids the pitfalls and misunderstandings associated with a word like 'independence'. The responsible selfhood of the Church is a much deeper thing than mere independence; we may perhaps define it as the Church's power, readiness and freedom to follow its divine call within its sphere of life.

In this definition three ideas are joined together. First, there is the thought of the Church's real power and freedom to follow its divine call. Foreign help, whether in money or in personal service, must always promote this power and freedom if it is not to injure the integrity and responsibility of the Church.

The emergence of the responsible Church as a result of the missionary's preaching of the Gospel to non-Christians is something for which all mission-boards must be prepared, and to which most of them look forward as the sign of God's blessing upon their labours, yet this event nearly always comes as a surprise. We have already noted the analogy of the family in this regard. It is easy to cry : 'No paternalism', but there is no doubt that even the slowest to acknowledge the maturity of the new generation is deeply concerned about that generation's welfare. No parent and no missionary will admit to desiring to retain authority for the sake of self-importance, and this is not always self-deception, though there may be error in the attitude of the older generation. 'We are but little children weak' at the beginning of our lives, and we continue to be a mixture of weakness and strength, immaturity and maturity, ignorance and wisdom, for a considerable time. The wise and loving parent is anxious to help his son to make the fullest possible preparation for life, and this is at the root of his apparent reluctance to recognize that the son has become a mature and responsible person.

Two common errors on the part of parents are, first, the error of imagining that development to maturity proceeds at the same pace in all persons, and, secondly, that of imagining that one's own views, shaped by one's own experience of life, are obviously correct, or at least that they deserve respect. In fact, as we all

Secondly, the definition reminds us that every church exists in a particular environment. Its members belong to this environment, at least as far as their physical existence is concerned, as citizens of this world, and it is in this environment first of all that the Church is called to exercise its missionary vocation. A missionary church must be an indigenous church, related to the soil and permeating society. Thirdly, the concept of responsibility, with its close association with autonomy and independence, implies freedom from outside influences and control which would hinder the Church from exercising its vocation. These influences may come from the parent churches or from secular powers.

The problem is presented by the tension between the indigenous Church and the foreign mission, and it is probable that the simplest expression of it would be in some such form as 'The responsible Church and the foreign Mission'. That could be, but need not necessarily be, narrower than the subject which is our present concern. We shall understand it as referring to the nature of the local church's responsibility to Christ, first and foremost; to other churches, whether 'older', 'younger' or 'contemporary', and to the world. This is obviously a problem for the Church as a whole, but we are specially concerned with the problem as it affects foreign missions and the churches associated with them.

know, some people mature more quickly than others, and one's own views are not infrequently quite mistaken, acknowledged by ourselves later in life to be so. Where the Church is concerned, these errors are to be considered still more seriously.

Above all else, we believe that the Church is not only the body of Christ, but the living Temple of His Spirit, and our Lord demands apparently few worldly qualifications for His Church. Numbers are unimportant—'where two or three are gathered together in My Name there am I in the midst of them'. Nor are worldly wealth and wisdom distinguishing marks of the Church. According to the New Testament the reverse would appear to be the case, as could be easily proved from a number of well-known texts. Again, the kind of development with which we are concerned in the Church is not merely cultural development, to be achieved through education and discipline. 'The wind bloweth where it listeth; so is everyone that is born of the Spirit.' Texts of Scripture come readily to the mind in this matter, but perhaps too readily.

Do we adequately solve a spiritual problem when we have brought up a text or two in support of one side or the other? 'The Devil can quote Scripture to his purpose.' Most easily can we adduce texts to our aid in support of a purely 'spiritual' view of life and of the Church, and yet such a view would be at variance with the most consistent emphasis of the Bible which is on an incarnational view of life. Man became a living soul, an embodied spirit. The Word of God was made flesh so that in Christ men beheld 'all the fullness of the Godhead under bodily conditions'. And the Church is His Body. If we take the incarnation seriously, and the Church as in some sense the extension of the Incarnation, and if we take seriously the incarnational principle in the life of every believer, we shall have to consider seriously both the spirit and the flesh, the divine and the human. We shall err if we ignore either fact in this mysterious union.

To treat a Church indefinitely as a 'younger Church', with the implication that the responsible selfhood of the Church is a matter of age in years, or, indeed, to speak of any believer so, is to ignore the mysterious operation of the Spirit. Equally distorted is the view that because of the gift of the Spirit to Christ's Church, any local congregation of simple believers is gifted with plenary inspiration and near-infallibility in all the manifold responsibilities which are laid upon it. This is a specially dangerous heresy where the churches in former 'mission fields' are concerned, responsible as they are, not only for pastoral and evangelistic activities, but also for a wide range of social work, including the management of schools and, in some cases, hospitals. The determining of the nature of the 'responsible selfhood of the Church', in these circumstances, is a matter of great complexity. 'Thank God,' said Martin Luther, 'any schoolchild knows what the Church is,' but the question of what is a responsible Church under these conditions, or at what stage it should be entrusted with responsibility, is one which has baffled Christian leaders in both East and West in our generation.

Dr. Beyerhaus' book is a contribution to the solution of the problems involved. He points out, for example, that some exponents of missionary principles have envisaged a lengthy process of education and discipline on the part of the young Church before it can be regarded, in the fullest sense of the term, as 'responsible'. Others have gone to the opposite extreme, in holding, or appearing to hold, that the moment a man is converted he is a fully responsible Christian, and that the moment he enters into a covenant relationship with other converts there springs into existence a fully responsible Church. Dr. Beyerhaus' careful analysis shows the error of both these views and attempts an appraisal of the responsible selfhood of the Church which avoids both the ignoring of the presence of the Spirit on the one hand and a naïve, almost mechanical, view of the Spirit's activity on the other.

In making his appraisal, Beyerhaus examines the actual circumstances of the origin and growth of the Church in certain areas, notably the Anglican Church in West Africa, particularly Nigeria, the German mission-field among the Batak people of Indonesia and the American Presbyterian field in Korea. These do not in any way exhaust the variety of circumstances under which this missionary problem is set. One could wish for a discussion of, say, the work of Congregationalist missionaries in South India, and of Baptists in the Congo, but the examples Dr. Beyerhaus gives are representative of three main types of church-tradition and missionary principles.

In all these examples, we have to face the theological and practical problems raised, not only by church-traditions imported from the West into non-Western countries, (the fact, noted by Bishop Sundkler, that 'all transplantation involves mutation') but also by non-theological factors like the development of nationalism in colonial and ex-colonial territories, with the consequent demand for the relating of the Church's life and doctrinal statements to local, indigenous cultural forms. This last factor raises the problem of the limits to which a Church can go in coming to terms with culture and remaining above all the world's cultures as a body which is not only historical but eschatological, not only national, related to the soil, but also international, ecumenical.

The ecumenical nature of the Church raises the question whether we are justified in concentrating on a purely local manifestation of the Church, either a local congregation or a regional grouping of congregations. Is any single congregation or group of believers properly called a Church, in isolation from the whole body of Christ? Much of the bitterness and frustration experienced in mission churches may be traced to too great an emphasis on particular groups considered as 'we' or 'they', instead of a recognition of such groups as members of the whole Body in which alone they have significance and the right to be called, albeit in a derivative sense only, 'churches'. There is only one Church, as there is only one Lord and one Faith, and this fact must colour all church-relations, especially those of 'giving' and 'receiving', and all claims to independence and autonomy.

Finally, whether we are considering the one Church, the *una sancta,* or the local congregation as an expression of that one Church in a particular area, we must never overlook the fact that the Church does not live for itself, for the nurture and fellowship of its own members. Mission is also one of its essential marks, no less than worship and fellowship. The Church exists to proclaim its Lord to the world and this is a world-wide task, directed towards every nation and to every aspect of the nation's life. Only in the light of this understanding of the Church can we begin to understand the nature of its responsible selfhood.

So, with this brief introduction, we turn to Dr. Beyerhaus' study of the *Responsible Church as a Missionary Problem.* This study was made under the guidance of Bishop Sundkler, when Professor of Missions at Upsala in Sweden.

Since its publication in 1956 the German edition has been received warmly as an important contribution to missionary thinking, and there have been suggestions from various quarters that the work should be translated into English and so made available to an even wider public. It is doubtful, however, whether a simple translation into English would be the most helpful means of communicating Dr. Beyerhaus' work to the English-reading public. It has been suggested that what would be more helpful would be an English presentation of Dr. Beyerhaus' material and thought, and the following is an attempt at such a presentation, less scholarly than the original but, it is hoped, easier for the ordinary reader, as distinct from the theological specialist, to understand, and at the same time faithful to Dr. Beyerhaus' own position. The historical sections have been much abbreviated, both those dealing with missionary theories and with the field examples, but they are presented, it is hoped, in sufficient fullness to make the concluding part of the work intelligible and forceful.

PART ONE

PIONEERS IN THE PRINCIPLES OF MISSIONS

Chapter 1

ANGLO-AMERICAN THEORIES

1. HENRY VENN OF THE CHURCH MISSIONARY SOCIETY

The Euthanasia of a Mission

THE Church Missionary Society has always been a denominational Society, even though it has shown a broad and sympathetic attitude to non-Anglican denominations. 'Church but not High Church' was how John Venn (Henry Venn's father) expressed his understanding of that Society's position. He himself, like most of his founding colleagues in the C.M.S., was a staunch Evangelical and, as Rector of Clapham in South London, gathered about him that company of kindred spirits who came to be nicknamed 'the Clapham sect'. So staunch an Evangelical was John Venn that it is said that he gave financial help to Evangelical dissenting ministers of chapels in country villages where the Anglican incumbent was known to belong to the 'High Church' party.

Evangelicals though the C.M.S. founders may have been, however, they were members of the Anglican Communion, and that Communion existed wherever there were Anglicans, certainly within the British Empire. Wherever the first C.M.S. missionaries went, unlike those of the London Missionary Society, they found that their Church had already gone before them, if only on paper. That is, they found themselves in an Anglican diocese, even though only a handful of the inhabitants—and they often entirely expatriates, in what might be an area many times the size of England—could properly be called Anglicans. The bishop was there, at any rate, and, from the start, there existed the question of the relation between him and the C.M.S. missionaries working in his diocese.

This question was not one which caused any considerable tension in the early days of the C.M.S. history. The Society was fairly generally accepted within the Church of England as a

25

voluntary organization of members of the Church. Henry Venn, as Secretary of the Society, expressed its position as being 'in subordination to Church authority but upon the basis of voluntary action'. But what if voluntary action on the part of men who believed themselves to be guided by the Spirit should, as it sometimes did, put them at variance with church-authority?

As the C.M.S. grew in strength and in the scope of its operations, it became increasingly urgent to find a solution of the problem how the Society's Constitution could be fitted into the Church of England, at home and in its colonial branches. The urgency was made all the greater by the rise of what might well be called 'militant clericalism', championed mainly by the High Church movement. Henry Venn began his work as Secretary of the Society during this head-on collision of Evangelicalism and High Anglicanism.

As soon as Henry Venn had taken over his duties, he devoted much energy to settling the dispute which, he saw, raised fundamental issues of missionary policy, apart altogether from any wider issues of church-life and thought. He did this by incorporating the Society more fully into the Church. Earlier, the C.M.S. founders had regarded themselves as 'spiritual men doing spiritual things', the implication apparently being that others were more responsible for administration.

Under Henry Venn's leadership, the Society limited its activities to what might be called temporal or lay functions. Venn lists these functions under four headings : 1. The collection and administration of funds for the work; 2. the selection and training of missionary candidates; 3. the sending of ordained missionaries to mission-stations, and 4. the supervision of the missionaries in their work among the non-Christian people. The 'spiritual' side of the work, that is, the arrangements for worship and pastoral care, and, as time went on, arrangements for the building up of an indigenous ministry; in fact, all that in the admittedly narrow sense, might be called 'church-work', is handed over to the local bishop.

This, secured by the insertion of a new clause in the Society's Constitution, enabled the bishops to accept the Society as a voluntary organization co-operating with them in their work, but it also implied that the Society was only the handmaid of the

Church, and that, as the Church grew, the work of the mission would be transformed, and might, or so Henry Venn thought, come to an end altogether. His famous expression 'the euthanasia of a Mission' represents a thought which is already foreshadowed in his earliest utterances as Secretary of the Society.

Many factors, not least a severe financial crisis which the C.M.S. suffered in 1841, the year in which Venn began his work as Secretary, served to emphasize the need to review the Society's policy, and, in particular, to create a 'native Church' which would be responsible for pastoral duties, leaving the missionaries free for pioneering evangelism. It was not that the development of an indigenous Church and ministry should be promoted in order to relieve the missionary society of financial burdens; the aim was rather that the Church should, for the sake of its own spiritual health and financial security, be made, as far as possible, independent of foreign support over which it had no control.

Venn saw, decades before it was at all widely appreciated, the essential evil of missionary paternalism which, in the name of affection, actually thwarted this development. All this led to his epoch-making aim, formulated as Point 10 of his Memorandum of 1851 : 'the settlement of a Native Church under Native Pastors upon a self-supporting system.' Venn realized that the 'native Church', on this basis, was still a distant goal, but he was to be disappointed that even his very modest expectations were not realized. His plans were frustrated by this very missionary paternalism which we have already mentioned, so that, ten years later, in 1861, he issued another Memorandum embodying stricter instructions to missionaries and a more fully worked out programme of church-development. Missionaries, he says, are to limit themselves to evangelistic work, and are not to become involved in church-administration—at least once the native Church is established.

To begin with, of course, the missionaries were necessary for uniting converts into groups which Venn called 'Christian companies' rather than churches. At that stage, the work was still part of the evangelistic work of the Society. The next step in transforming these companies into churches is taken when the missionary considers the groups' contributions are sufficiently high to support a native minister. At that point, the missionary raises

27

the group to the status of a 'Native Pastorate under an ordained Native, paid for by the Native Church Fund'. This minister, however, is still responsible to the missionary as long as the national church fund is administered and subsidized by the missionary society. The third phase in the development of the indigenous Church comes when groups of native pastorates meet together regularly in a District Church Conference. Missionaries are to attend this Conference along with native ministers, but, says Venn, 'when any considerable District has been thus provided for by an organized native Church, the foreign agency will have no place in the work and that District will have been fully prepared for a Native Episcopate.' This, however, is only the beginning.

Venn observes :

'If the elementary principles of self-support and self-government and self-extension (here he mentions for the first time the third constituent of his formula) be thus sown with the seed of the Gospel, we may hope to see the healthy growth and expansion of the Native Church'.

At this stage, he says, the missionary will be able to resign all pastoral work into the hands of the native congregations under their own pastors, and gradually relax his superintendence over the pastors themselves 'till it insensibly ceases'. Then the missionary and all missionary agency are to be transferred to the 'regions beyond', new unevangelized fields. As far as the former field is concerned, the mission has completed its work; in Venn's words 'the euthanasia of the Mission' has taken place.

It is easy for us today to point to inadequacies, and even possible errors, in Venn's judgement. We may question the rightness of his apparently sole criterion of self-support for church-recognition, and still more may we question whether the mission's responsibility ceases altogether when the local Church has emerged and become fully organized on a self-supporting and self-governing basis. But Venn's insights were revolutionary in his day. He sees self-support as a genuine mark of life created by the Spirit, because he is convinced that financial sacrifices enable the young Church to show its eagerness and the reality of its incorporation into the Body of Christ. If he seems to us to assume too readily that the missionary task is finished when the new Church is established, that is due not to any lack of concern for 'native Christians' but, on the contrary, to his conviction that as long as they are supervised by the mission they cannot come of age, nor gain spiritual maturity. Becoming a new Church, he considered, is a spiritual stage superior to that where Christians are the objects of missionary rule.

We must ask, however, whether Venn's solution was fully adequate. His demand for missionary mobility was a step in the right direction; but were the heathen needing missionary care only to be found in the 'regions beyond'? Who could guarantee that the Church would really extend its scope in districts where foreign missions regarded their own task as completed? It remains doubtful whether Venn's confidence was justified, and whether there was not rather the danger that the young Church would devote all its energies to preserving its own self-government and self-support.

Venn thought he had safeguarded the mobility of the missionary, but was this at the cost of a static Church? Richter, the great German missionary historian, notes several decades of stagnation in Anglican churches in India, subsequent to Venn's reforms, and he attributes this to Venn's missionary theory. If a small band of heathen converts is surrounded by a large majority of heathen, he says, it is unwise to allow this group of congregations to concentrate exclusively on their own ecclesiastical interests, as this would paralyse their own missionary spirit and energies.

Venn had no intention of leaving the congregations to stagnate. Nor was he naïvely optimistic about the powers of the young churches, for he had already observed signs of stagnation among the South Indian Christians associated with the C.M.S. As an Evangelical, however, he believed firmly in the operation of the Holy Spirit, which could not finally be frustrated by man's laxity and self-centredness. In his well-known letter to the Bishop of Jamaica he acknowledges that his whole system becomes effective only through the operation of the Holy Spirit acting in the hearts of men. Further, as a Churchman and an Anglican, he believes that the native bishop will be not a solitary figure, but an integral part of the responsible leadership within the whole Anglican Communion, or, as he would have said, 'the Church of England'. Within this Communion, too, the Missionary Society plays a significant part.

Even if the Society has handed over administrative responsibility to the new Church, and its local missionaries have moved on to regions beyond, because of its place within the framework of the church-organization in England and its ties of warm affection with the new Church in the former 'mission field', it serves as a connecting link between the Church in England and the Church in, for example, India. Venn is looking beyond his own day, far beyond the older static colonial conception of missions as outposts of the Church of England. His 'Native Episcopal Church' may be a branch of the Church of England, but it is also to be a responsible Church, responsible not least for out-reach into the non-Christian world around it.

It was Venn's great contribution that, after a long period of patriarchal, individualistic missionary work, he pointed the way to a 'church-centric' mission. He left unsolved, however, the problem with which we are still grappling today, namely, the relation of the foreign missionary to the mission of the Church overseas. The fact that this problem is still unsolved suggests that Venn need not be blamed for failing to solve it more than a century ago. By his emphasis on the Church, and his equally strong emphasis on mission, he at any rate set some of the terms of the problem. The phrase 'euthanasia of a Mission' does less than justice to his view as a whole. It applies only to the patriarchal stage of the foreign missionary's relation to the newly converted Christians. Venn saw clearly, far more clearly than some people do even today, that if the Church is truly planted in a given area, that Church is the organ of Christ's Mission to the world around. Churches and individual Christians elsewhere, called to take part in Christ's Mission in that area, can do so only in the name of the Church there. But how this is to be effected Venn does not say.

2. RUFUS ANDERSON OF THE AMERICAN BOARD

The self-propagating Church

While Henry Venn was directing the affairs of the Church Missionary Society in London and making his great contribution to the Principles of Missions, the American Congregationalist

Rufus Anderson was performing very similar functions in Boston. The two great Mission Secretaries had many things in common and kept up a warm friendship over many years. They influenced one another's thinking to such an extent that it is not easy to decide which of them first conceived the missionary objective of a native church administering, supporting and propagating itself.

It is more important for this present study, perhaps, to note where the two men differed in their missionary principles, rather than to note the very wide area of their agreement. Thus, for Venn the Anglican, it was obvious that mission-churches, when they became autonomous, should be grouped together in dioceses. For Anderson the Congregationalist, the term 'Church' meant essentially the local congregation. Congregationalists in Britain and America laid great stress on the autonomy, under Christ, of the local congregation. It is not, therefore, surprising that missionaries of their tradition should make this same emphasis on the 'mission field'. This was based, not on any philosophy of human rights, but on a theology which stressed human responsibility to God with whom the individual believed himself to be in a personal relation. Thus, for Anderson the discovery of the necessary autonomy of the mission-churches was perhaps easier than it was for Venn, although we must remember their common Evangelical tradition.

Perhaps it was the very depth of Anderson's Congregationalist principles that caused him to resist certain trends which he noted in areas where missionaries of the 'American Board' were working. These missionaries may have been equally convinced Congregationalists, like Anderson himself, but what Anderson found, in the course of Secretarial visits to India and later to Hawaii, was that the educational institutions had been developed out of all proportion to the strength of the local congregations. Some of the schools which he saw on his travels seemed to him to have no evangelistic value, or even Christian influence, and these he closed. He noted in India that, in the forty years during which the Mission had been working there, not a single Indian Christian had been ordained to the ministry. This was very probably connected with the emphasis laid by the missionaries on the work of institutions, but it seemed to Anderson that missionary paternalism was also responsible for the weakness of church-leadership.

He observed dryly that 'missionaries might be more forward than they have been to throw responsibility on their native converts and preachers'.

The reforms which Anderson introduced after his visit to India were directed away from the institutions and the mission 'compounds' towards the formation of rural churches, with Indian ministers and an Indian District Council. Missionaries were not to be represented on these Councils, but were to carry on their work as an independent body.

Anderson carried through similar reforms in the very different field of Hawaii, where the Board declared the local church-organization autonomous, and encouraged not only a considerable increase in the number of native pastors, but also the Church's responsibility for a foreign mission, in its turn. Nevertheless, in Hawaii there was this difference, that owing to the backwardness of the local native congregations—as distinct from American settlers on the island—missionaries were to be closely associated with the Church and its Councils, even though the Church was technically autonomous. In fact, bowing to the logic of the situation in Hawaii, Anderson went so far as to rule that the missionary should maintain a 'common relation' to all local churches founded by him, as their 'ecclesiastical father and adviser'. If this seems to contradict his own principle of church-autonomy, to say nothing of Congregationalist principles generally, Anderson argued that the situation was a special one (though very general on the mission field!) and the arrangement suggested a purely temporary expedient.

In theory Anderson seems to take a different line from Venn, for whom autonomy is the last stage of ecclesiastical development. He argues that St. Paul established churches after a surprisingly short time, and that these were, from their inception, 'autonomous'. In practice, there does not seem to be so much difference between the policies of the two men, for Anderson is forced by experience to recognize that the initial weakness of young churches leaves room for a scheme of development towards independence. He believes that this development should be as rapid as possible. He certainly has no idea of perpetuating any kind of missionary *episcopé* in the young Church. But, in fact, the period lasted for several generations, during which the local churches of the American Board in Hawaii and in India obviously needed the supra-congregational supervision of missionaries. Here, it must be admitted, there is a noticeable gap between Anderson's theory and his practice.

Anderson's main emphasis, however, is on mission, not on church organization. This is seen in the priorities indicated by his description of the Church as, first, self-propagating, secondly, self-governing, and, thirdly, self-supporting. This is exactly the reverse order to that given by Venn who did not, in fact, as we have seen, mention the term self-propagating in his first statement of policy. It is in the context of his passionate desire to evangelize that we are to understand his belief that mission churches ought to be rendered autonomous. For Venn the constitution of autonomous churches means setting the missionary free for his own proper evangelistic task. For Anderson, on the other hand, the young local churches themselves are means towards the evangelistic end. 'Missions,' he says in his *Outlines of Missionary Policy*, as early as 1856, 'are instituted for the spread of a scriptural, self-propagating Christianity. This is their only aim.'

3. ROLAND ALLEN AND THE WORLD-DOMINION MOVEMENT

The Mission of the Spirit

It would be unduly pessimistic to regard Venn and Anderson as 'voices crying in the wilderness'. Both were Secretaries of great Mission Boards, which not only gave them a sympathetic hearing, but also attempted to put their ideas into practice. Radical changes, of course, cannot easily be introduced over-night, and we have seen how Anderson himself accepted the need for an *interim* period, with his three-fold principle as a distant goal. In fact, the principle was very widely accepted in this sense, and in this sense the ideal was very largely immunized. The sting of its challenge was drawn by the acceptance of the principle, as a distant goal. There was the subtle temptation to imagine that the principle had already been introduced because, in principle, it had been accepted, and, in the *interim* period of uncertain duration, to continue, in practice, with the patriarchal missionary methods of the pre-Venn-era.

A small band of missionaries and their supporters, at the beginning of the present century, irritatingly insisted on taking the principle as something to be put into practice at once. Naturally these men were dismissed by many as 'doctrinaire idealists', but in fact they were men of practical experience, and, in the case of at least one of them, of some theological competence. Out of their meeting together, and common convictions regarding missionary strategy, grew the World Dominion Movement. This Movement, through its Press, responsible for an important missionary periodical and for a series of church surveys, and its associate organization the Survey Application Trust (founded in 1924), for the last forty years has conducted pioneer surveys of evangelistic opportunities in different parts of the world and has sought to indicate how these can best be met.

The founders of the World Dominion Movement were all specially connected with China, although they explained that the principles which they expounded were of world-wide application. One was Thomas Cochrane, a London Missionary Society medical missionary in China, who had already, in 1913, published a survey of missionary methods in that country, emphasizing the unequal distribution of missionary workers there, both as between one area and another and also between one department of work and another.

It was this survey which brought Cochrane into contact with Sydney Clark, a former successful business man, who, as a result of his interest in the L.M.S. work in China, had retired at the early age of forty-five in order to devote all his time to the study of missionary methods. Though of humble origin and of little formal education, Clark proved in the sphere of missions, as he had earlier done in the business world, to have a penetrating mind and sound judgement in practical affairs. As a business man, he was horrified at the incompetence shown in the practical administration of missionary work, particularly of missionary institutions and, as a man of great evangelistic zeal, he was equally horrified by the great gulf apparently fixed between these institutions set in the static mission compounds—appropriately called 'stations' —and the world-wide evangelistic task of the Church which, he felt, was being neglected. During the years 1910-13 he had planned a world missionary survey to prove his contention that, through unbusiness-like methods and misdirected energy, the world missionary task had not yet been fulfilled, in spite of the high hopes, the prayers and sacrificial giving of its supporters through over a century. It was this survey that brought him into touch with Cochrane.

These two Congregationalist laymen were joined by the Anglo-Catholic priest, Roland Allen, who had spent eight years with the Society for the Propagation of the Gospel in China, from 1895 to 1903. After his early retirement owing to ill-health, Allen had continued his theological and missionary studies with a firm conviction that missionary methods must be grounded on biblical insights. It was his study of the New Testament which led him to criticize the missionary methods of his own day in one of his earliest, but still widely read books—*Missionary Methods—St. Paul's or Ours?*[1] In this he expressed some of the convictions which he had reached during his missionary service, notably his confidence that local churches could exhibit considerable life and also provide unsuspected economic resources for the work if their sense of responsibility were awakened.

The greatest hindrance to the development of a responsible Church Allen believed to be missionary paternalism. 'A visit of two or three weeks stirs up a Church', he wrote to the S.P.G. from China, 'long continued residence stifles it.' There is obviously a good deal of exaggeration in some of Allen's statements (K. S. Latourette has indicated some of the errors in his New Testament conclusions in a sober article in the *International Review of Missions* for April 1953) but the neglect of his teaching, until the last few years, was due not so much to a critical examination of his work leading to an adverse judgement upon it, as to prejudice and, probably, 'vested interests'. This neglect and disparagement of his work greatly depressed Allen, and he was on the point of giving up all hope of making an impression when, in 1920, Sydney Clark pressed him to join him and Thomas Cochrane in their deliberations on missionary policy.

Clark had been led by Allen's *Missionary Methods* to the conviction that the principle of self-support, to which he had himself

[1] World Dominion Press: Price 12s 6d.

35

long subscribed, pre-supposed freedom from missionary control. It was Clark's money which financed the Survey Application Trust in 1924. He conceived the World Dominion Movement and, again, provided its economic basis. Cochrane was the indefatigable propagator who turned the principles of his colleagues into practicable plans, while Allen became the theological leader of the movement which owed much of its impetus to the biblical basis and the logical conviction of his numerous publications. The methods which Allen advocated are meaningless apart from the theology out of which they arose.

There is obviously much in common between Allen and the earlier missionary thinkers Venn and Anderson. Where he differs from them, particularly from Venn, is, perhaps, in his conviction that, instead of granting ecclesiastical autonomy as the last stage of a long process of development, it should be granted to the new Church at the very beginning, as soon as it can be properly called a Church. Referring to St. Paul, he says :

'He withheld no gift from them which might enable them to dispense with his presence; He gave as a right to the Spirit-bearing Body the powers which duly belong to a Spirit-bearing Body.'

The emphasis on the Holy Spirit in this passage is typical of Allen's missionary outlook. Indeed, his conception of the Holy Spirit influenced his missionary principles more than did his High Church background, although he laid much stress on the efficacy of the Sacraments, which, he believed, guaranteed that the Church remained a visible Body. He is no 'spiritualist', in the sense in which that term is sometimes used of Anabaptists and similar groups. For him, the Church is firmly planted in the sphere of flesh and blood, but it is permeated and quickened by the Spirit. Allen particularly stressed the life-giving, dynamic function of the Spirit, rather than the Spirit as giver of wisdom and understanding. He believed that missionaries had laid too much stress on the Spirit as 'the Giver of wisdom and understanding', and that this had led them to be over-anxious about the young churches' doctrinal orthodoxy. This, in turn, led the missionary to regard himself as the indispensable safeguard of correct teaching and thus to be reluctant to give the Church autonomy.

Allen's stress on the dynamic function of the Spirit, coupled with his High Church sacramental doctrine, led him to regard the Church's 'inherent vitality' as the decisive factor. Thus his practical solution of the problem of the responsible Church is identical with that of his Congregationalist friend Clark, whose aspirations for the independent mission-Church were summed up in the words : 'But the Church must be living, for only a living thing has this sustaining and propagating power.'

In many World Dominion publications, 'self-support' stands for full autonomy. This does not mean, however, that the financial is the chief aspect : 'self-support' in this context has a spiritual meaning. Allen feels that the missionary societies have done more harm than good to the young churches with their money. He goes so far as to say that their methods are not essentially unlike medieval conversions by the sword, only the sword has been replaced by money. Both methods savour of imperialism. He is not suggesting that missionaries have bribed individuals to accept the Christian faith, but he believes that in their employment of vast financial resources with which to spread the Gospel and build up the Church, missions have introduced a corrupting and unspiritual element. In particular, missions, he says, have hindered the Church from being acknowledged as self-supporting, through their own standards of what this is thought to involve.

In fact, Allen says, the young Church is fully self-supporting, from the beginning. It has all the spirit of power needed for its life; it has ministers empowered to preach, to administer the Sacraments and to ordain. What it does not possess is the wealth of the Western churches enabling it to support a full-time paid ministry, on Western lines. But why should it be assumed that this is the only form of ministry in the Church? Allen believes such a ministry is beyond the resources of most local churches, and the demand that they should have such a ministry only deprives them of their right to be autonomous. Where the Church with difficulty supports a full-time paid minister, the tendency is for it to become introverted, spending its energies on self-support, i.e., the support of a professional ministry, instead of concentrating on its principle task, which is to spread the Gospel. This again is an exaggeration, but every missionary will recognize the truth included in Allen's words.

So, Allen rejects the famous three-stages theory in the so-called process of devolution, and holds that the first band of native Christians, who have found Jesus Christ and received the Holy Spirit, is to be regarded as an autonomous native Church. This Church, again, is from the start a true missionary agent. Self-propagation is not merely an educational aim of the missionary who founds a Church and wants to show it what a true Church ought to be. It results spontaneously from the outpouring of the Holy Spirit. Mission is not just the result of obedience to the missionary command, but of a free impulse caused by the new life. Allen calls this phenomenon 'the spontaneous expansion of the Church', and defines it as 'the expansion which follows the irresistible attraction of the Christian Church for men who see its ordered life and are drawn to it by desire to discover the secret of life which they instinctively desire to share'. That this process has taken place is the only important and unfailing proof that a young Church has become 'indigenous'.

On the question of the foreign missionary's relation to the indigenous Church, Allen is inclined at first to be negative. He does not believe, he says, that the world should be evangelized by 'foreigners'—presumably where a local Church already exists. He thinks the missionary should give up the control of the young Church. But he is not wholly negative. The missionary is pre-eminently the pioneer, founding more and more local churches, but, as such, his role is a transient and diminishing one. 'Each missionary ought to work as if he were to have no successor.' But, with Clark, he is convinced that just as a mother leaves hold of her child in teaching it to walk, but does not desert the child, so the missionary will be available to further the interests of the Church whilst never obtruding his help, and he believes the new converts will welcome this. He does not, however, discuss the economic as well as the psychological factors which make this relation so difficult for both parties. 'Your doctrine is too high for this wicked world,' one missionary wrote to him. Perhaps it is, but for the rest of his life, both in the context of foreign missions and after his unhappy break with Thomas Cochrane and the World Dominion Movement, in relation to the Church in England, Allen continued to press for a proper recognition of the power of the Holy Spirit and for a form of ministry that took that power seriously.

The influence of the World Dominion Movement, and of Allen's teaching in particular, was only slight for many years. Tradition was too powerful. Today, Allen's writings are studied more than ever. His *Missionary Methods* has passed through five editions since the war and is read as eagerly by young churches (the Church of South India has called for a Tamil translation) as by leaders of Western mission-boards. His work is especially popular in those missionary circles in the West labelled 'Conservative Evangelical'. It is probably true to say, however, that many of his present admirers overlook his emphasis on the sacramental aspect of the Church's life, and wrongly understand his emphasis on the Holy Spirit to imply a negative 'spiritualizing' attitude to organized Christianity.

The veterans of the World Dominion Movement find themselves today in an embarrassing position. Under pressure of world politics (partly at least) a modified version of their demands for reform has been universally adopted and put into practice. On the other hand, it does not seem possible to reaffirm Allen's and Clark's original radical conception. In our present situation it is exceptional for a missionary to be called for genuine 'pioneer' work. The relation between 'Mission' and 'Inter-Church Aid' is closer than ever, for 'the Church is the Mission'. Finally, in this ecumenical era in which young church-organizations in Asia and Africa stand at the side of the older churches, it seems an anachronism to stress that the first small local church in a country ought to be regarded as the indigenous Church there.

The nature of the 'responsible Church' has to be considered now, not only in relation to foreign missions, but also to national churches, whose central councils may well seem to some simple folk just as remote as overseas mission-boards and hardly less foreign. But Allen and his friends sought to solve the problems of their own day, not of ours.

4. J. MERLE DAVIS

The Economic and Social Problem

Each of the missionary thinkers we have so far considered based his thoughts on the Bible and Christian experience. Henry

Venn, the Evangelical Anglican, looks for men 'who know the experience of spiritual conversion and who will accordingly cease from the love of this world and offer themselves to Christ, willing to spend and be spent for Him'. With such men as missionaries, converts will also show similar graces and undergo a first-hand spiritual experience which will make it impossible for them to be merely dependents of the missionary. Nor will the missionary wish his converts to be dependent upon him; rather will he welcome them as fellow-members of the Body of Christ, the community of the redeemed, and look for spiritual fruits from them. These fruits will include the grace of responsibility before God, and one expression of this will be self-support, for Venn, as we have seen, a genuine if not essential criterion of life in the Spirit.

Anderson, in his theory of missions, starts from his Congregationalist principle of the personal relation and responsibility of the individual before God, and proceeds at once from that point to responsibility for mission; that is, for the spread of 'scriptural, self-propagating Christianity'. This is the kernel of Christian responsibility, and he is concerned with other forms of responsibility, e.g., for self-government and self-support, only within this context. In his most important book *Foreign Missions: Their relations and their Claims* he seeks to develop this teaching theologically, in accordance with his own understanding of the New Testament with its call for world-wide evangelization in preparation for the imminent coming of the Kingdom. It is on this basis that he conducts his critical review of missionary institutions and emphasizes that the power of God will endow the young churches with vitality, both for mission and for self-government.

Roland Allen, the Anglo-Catholic, is no less convinced of the reality of the Holy Spirit's power which makes the young Church responsible for church-discipline, spiritual progress and the spread of the Gospel, a conviction which he justifies from the New Testament record of St. Paul's own 'missionary methods'.

Theological considerations lie at the root of the important teaching of another American missionary scholar, Dr. J. Merle Davis, whose book *New Buildings on Old Foundations* (1947) has had much influence on the study of the Responsible Church in the last decade. Davis, however, is specially concerned with the economic and social factors which 'challenge the Gospel of Christ and limit the growth of His Kingdom among Younger Churches'. As Director of the 'Department of Social and Economic Research' (founded by the International Missionary Council at its Jerusalem meeting in 1928) he was well qualified to deal with this aspect of missions, and his reports *The Economic and Social Environment of the Younger Churches* and *The Economic Basis of the Church* (Tambaram Report Vol. V) are seminal documents in this sphere. He is a typical representative of that trend in American theology which emphasizes the social significance of the Gospel, but this does not mean that he teaches only a 'social Gospel'.

Davis starts with the prosaic but disquieting fact that, after a century-and-a-half of Protestant missions, only 15 per cent of the 55,000 local churches have achieved a minimum of self-support. That means : the majority of Protestant mission-churches are still controlled by foreign missionary societies which in their turn—as Venn was the first to point out—are hampered in their proper evangelistic work by this burden of responsibility. He does not feel hopeless about this depressing conclusion from missionary statistics, but regards the missionary situation as partly conditioned by historical factors which man can understand and abolish.

He not only gives a diagnosis of the situation, but also suggests a remedy. Personal observation confronted him with the fact of the vastly different standards of living of the great masses of people in the East and of those of the Western nations. Many factors contribute to the appalling poverty of these masses, but Davis believes that this poverty need not be an insuperable obstacle to the financial independence of the younger churches.

He argues that Western missions have failed to meet this situation redemptively because they have been too 'Western' in their outlook, above all in submitting to what he calls the typically Western attitude of 'economic determinism', the belief in the determining influence of money in every sphere of life. Because of this, he says, communities like the backward classes in India, which have been kept for centuries in a spirit of dependence, have taken that spirit into the Christian Church. The Western missions, with their financial resources and fixed ideas about church-support, ministry and organization, far from emancipating converts from these communities from their traditional spirit of dependence, have actually fostered this spirit among them by laying upon them burdens they could not possibly bear unaided.

This, says Davis, has resulted in the 'mission compound mentality' which involved an acceptance of foreign (i.e., Western) patterns which are excessively elaborate and expensive, a disregard of indigenous patterns of organization and culture, and a lack of interest in social concerns, particularly for alleviating the distress which existed in the countries in which the Church was planted. In short, the Christians have retreated into a kind of *ghetto* instead of seeking to redeem society and proclaim the Gospel, not only to individuals but to nations. The Church, through the influence of the missions, offered no real substitute for the traditional social order. It simply substituted one form of dependence for another.

Davis is convinced, however, that every Church has the inner and external resources for economic self-support. This is no merely doctrinaire, abstract judgement : he bases his view on the experience of certain missions, personally known to him, which have not fallen into the general error of Western missionary policy, but which, dealing with the same kind of backward peoples, but following wiser methods, have enabled churches to achieve almost complete economic and, with it, spiritual autonomy. These churches are, above all, in his opinion and experience, the Batak Church, the Korean Church, the Karen Church and the Church in Angola. Which, then, is the right missionary method?

First of all, Davis accepts certain theological or spiritual principles as the necessary presuppositions for any economic theory of the Church's life. Here he is much influenced by the World Dominion Movement with which he came into contact, particularly through Clark's book *The Indigenous Church* (1928). To this book he owed the conception of the fourfold source of the Church's life :

1. Above all, the Church depends on its members' direct communion with God, the Giver of all life, and this communion is offered directly to all; 2. the younger church finds sustenance in the Word of God, the bread of life; 3. the common life of the Body of Christ enables the members of His Church to encourage, in-

struct and help one another in all kinds of ways without imposing their wills upon one another; 4. every member of the Church, from the moment of his conversion, has a field of service in the Church's life, and it is the responsibility of those already in the Church to find a place for him in its service.

Spiritual life, according to Davis, then, is the direct dependence of the young Church, and of every one of its members, upon God, with no necessity for human intermediaries like foreign missionaries after the Church is formed. This is, of course, a theological truth, but the matter is sometimes rather obscured in Davis' writings, owing to his emphasis on the social aspect of the Church's work. At times, it appears as if all that he is saying is that 'God helps those who help themselves', but the Divine power is presupposed in his economic and social teaching. It is as if he were saying : 'Given sensible methods of missionary work and self-reliance upon the part of the congregation, these alone would result in immense strides in church responsibility : how much more then is it possible to make such advance in dependence upon God !'

It is perhaps true to say that, as a sociologist, Davis specially emphasizes the human responsibilities, but it would be unfair to assume that this implies any failure to appreciate the spiritual reality of the Church. This is clear from the use he makes of the saying of the Chinese philosopher Hu Shih : 'Spiritual and material forces are the two wings of a bird which, in order to rise from the earth, needs the control of and the harmony between both wings'. Very naturally, Davis felt he had nothing specially original to say regarding the 'spiritual' or 'theological' wing : as a skilled and experienced sociologist he confines himself to discussing the 'material' wing.

He offers some very practical advice on the subject of mission subsidies in relation to church contributions. These, he thinks, should be on a fifty-fifty basis, the missionary society contributing only as much as the local Church raises from its own resources. An even more drastic suggestion is that the society should subsidize the mission Church only in the case of a new and promising project, and that the Church should be wholly self-supporting for its ordinary budget. This, Davis freely recognizes, would require a great deal of financial training on the part of the Church. One of the greatest pieces of service the mission can render is to teach the Church how to give. The great mistake has been that missions have been readier to give than to train in giving.

Missionaries must help the Church to draw its economic vitality from its native soil and so, not only to support itself, but to show the people around it how to overcome their age-old social and economic distress. For this work it will be necessary to train some missionaries for special work in rural areas. Missionaries must co-operate with Governments and other secular bodies, but, above all, they must co-operate with other missionaries, of other church-traditions, in what must be an ecumenical onslaught on rural indebtedness and dependence. The new building of the Church must be based, on its material side, on the old foundations of indigenous culture and local communal ties.

What Davis doesn't make sufficiently clear is how the two 'wings' are related to each other. Too often he speaks as if the local environment itself was the foundation on which the Church is to be built. He seems to interpret the Church's life in terms of the laws of psychology, sociology and economics. This, however, is due to his conviction, held in grief and pain, that the Christian missions, by disregarding social distress, have not only neglected to make visible the Kingdom of God which Jesus taught and demonstrated, but, like the Scribes and Pharisees whom Jesus condemned, have actually prevented others from entering in to its life. Davis would say it was an adequate task for him to make this plain, leaving the more 'eschatological' aspects of the Kingdom to others to deal with.

So far, we have discussed English and American teaching on missionary principles and the responsible Church. The next chapter will consider some aspects of Continental teaching, less diversified in denominational tradition and missionary strategy.

Chapter 2

THE GERMAN CONCEPT OF THE
NATIONAL CHURCH

1. GUSTAV WARNECK (1834-1910)

Independent National Churches the aim of Missions

GUSTAV WARNECK has been called the founder of the scientific study of missionary principles. Even before him, other Lutheran theologians had given attention to missionary methods, particularly in opposition to the pietistic principle that the purpose of missions was not the conversion of nations, but of individuals, 'brands plucked from the burning' as it were, to be gathered together into congregations of the faithful called out of the world. Against this pietistic principle, associated, for example, with the Moravian von Zinzendorf, men like Karl Graul, founder of the Leipzig Missionary Society, declared that the ultimate aim of Lutheran missions was to found a national Church (German *Volkskirche*), an indigenous Church in which the national character and social relations were to be preserved. Another Lutheran, Grundemann, went further and claimed the goal of missions to be nothing less than the 'Christianization of the nations'.[1] Warneck's main contribution to the theology of mission was his attempt to combine the salvation of individuals and the Christianizing of nations.

Warneck was also under the influence of a third tradition: that of mission, as being involved in the building up of an autonomous native Church, such as we have already seen in the teaching of Venn and Anderson, with whose writings he was familiar. If the English and American thinkers stressed the

It is of interest to note that the 'Basic Aim' of the London Missionary Society, adopted in 1795, was 'the preaching of the Gospel to heathen and other unenlightened nations'. We may not care for the epithets today but the aim of evangelization, not just of individuals but of nations, remains a 'basic aim' of the Church, essential to the character of the Christian Mission.

45

'autonomous' nature of the young churches, Warneck specially stressed their indigenous character as churches related to the soil of the country in which they were planted. He became the architect, so to speak, of the young churches planted by German missionaries, especially of the Batak Church in which his own son was working.

Warneck's starting point is the missionary command of the Risen Christ Himself : 'Go ye and make disciples of all nations'. A disciple is a believer who trusts the words of Jesus, has faith in His Person and lives according to His commands. But, holds Warneck, a disciple is not made 'overnight', in the instant of conversion, as the Pietists held. Warneck understands the New Testament term 'make disciples'—*Matheteuein*—as involving a process, through many stages of development, until the convert becomes a perfect disciple, in Paul's words a 'complete' man, having attained the measure of the stature of the fullness of Christ. Some disciples never attain this stage. Even St. Paul declined to claim that he himself had done so, but, he writes, 'I follow after'. A disciple is one who follows the Lord, 'pressing on to the mark, the ultimate goal of the full realization of the high calling in Christ Jesus'.

It follows from this conviction, in which the pietistic ideal of conversion is linked with the concept of Christianization, that for Warneck a congregation of the newly baptized is not yet a Church in the fullest sense. Its members are still just 'children beginning to be taught by Jesus'. The main lessons are still to follow. Here Warneck's theology of mission differs materially from that of Venn and Anderson, who held that the young Church was ready for self-government from the outset because it had, at any rate, a nucleus of the faithful. This difference was bound to have important results as the concept of 'autonomy' was developed further.

Who are to be made disciples—individuals or nations? In his classic work *Evangelische Missionslehre* (*Evangelical Theory of Mission*) Warneck maintains that there is, in fact, no contradiction between these two objectives. It is not a question of 'either—or', but one goal : the Christianizing of the nations follows the conversion of individuals. The Church, as 'a little flock' of those already converted, is God's instrument for the Christianizing of the nation, not a 'garden walled around', keeping itself separated from the main stream of the country's life. At the same time, he holds the national Church to be a kind of school which instructs and familiarizes the nation with the Gospel, teaching the masses and leading them to Christ.

The national Church provides a kind of framework within which the hidden or invisible Church, known only to God, can be built up like a cathedral within its scaffolding, for all men to see. Nevertheless, the national Church consists of local congregations and Warneck believes that these should achieve autonomy. He doesn't consider autonomy an 'essential mark' of the Church, as he feels his Anglo-American friends tended to do, but it is, for him, a mark of the mature Church. Autonomy, we may say, belongs to the *bene esse*, rather than to the *esse* of the Church. 'Even if this autonomy has not yet been achieved', he writes, 'and in a mission field where complete independence of the parent Church can never be achieved, the training for it and even the attempt to train converts for it are blessings.' The independence of the young Church, he argues, is as important for the Christians engaged in mission as for their converts. It will set the missionaries free for evangelistic work elsewhere, as Venn had argued, and also, says Warneck, it will help the growing Church towards self-propagation. It is essential, then, both for the spread of the Gospel and for the building up of a responsible Church, that the new Christians should gradually be set free from the missionaries' leading strings and be led to responsibility and initiative.

As his thinking progressed, Warneck subjected the concept of church-autonomy to ever-closer examination, and the difference between his outlook and the Anglo-American point of view became increasingly clear. Both his own thought and his knowledge of the aberrations of certain 'autonomous' churches (like the Congregationalists in Japan, who, in an excess of nationalistic zeal and for no other reason, demanded the withdrawal of the American missionaries) led him to condemn the views of men like Venn and Anderson as 'independentist'. He became convinced of the danger to the true life of the Church if 'excessive independentist zeal' and a doctrinaire theory of missions put into practice the principles of self-government, self-support and self-propagation without regard to what was right for the actual circumstances.

Warneck does not object to the principles themselves, but to their blind and unsuitable application. So he advises missionaries to proceed slowly and carefully in the application of these principles, and to be more concerned with the training and building up of the Church than with rash attempts to treat it as fully grown, regardless of its actual stage of development. He believes that there can be no autonomy in the Church except on a firm biblical foundation, a life firmly rooted in indigenous culture and with the leadership of steadfast, trained and committed people.

Warneck particularly stresses the facts of the Church's unity and continuity. He deplores the introduction of Western denominational differences into mission churches, and he believes that these churches should be taught only 'basic creeds' like the Apostles' Creed, plus some simple but distinctly Protestant statement of faith. He says : 'No Church is autonomous in the sense of having its origin in itself; its faith has been brought to it from outside, and it can become autonomous only by making this faith its very own'.

Warneck lays very great stress on the need for the Church to be truly indigenous. Five things, he says, need to be borne in mind when laying the foundations of a new Church. First, the mother-tongue must be used in church, school and in any training institution. Secondly, natural social ties, above all, those of the family, must be preserved and strengthened in the process of christianization, not broken. He even goes so far as to say that, as the house-congregation is the basis of the community-church, baptism ought, if possible, to be postponed until all members of the family are converted. Social relations are to be permeated with the leaven of the Gospel so that, ideally, the whole community joins the Church in a body. Thirdly, Christians are not to be isolated in a mission compound system, for they become impotent if they are uprooted from their natural environment. Fourthly, when founding a Church, the missionaries are to concentrate not on the lower but on the middle classes, for these, Warneck maintains, are the sound core of society. Lastly, any folk customs which are not spiritually incompatible with the Christian religion are to be preserved with imagination and warm-heartedness.

Further, for the building up of a responsible Church it is essential, says Warneck, to have the co-operation of local Christians, as teachers, evangelists and ministers, as well as church officers and other voluntary workers. There can be no independent indigenous Church, he argues, without self-support, although self-support of itself does not make a responsible Church. He rejects the argument that self-support is of itself a sufficient guarantee of responsibility and quotes the example of the Rhenish Mission churches in South Africa which were financially independent but lacked local leaders.

Warneck says very little about the third criterion in Venn's formula, namely that the responsible Church should be self-propagating. This is partly due to his particular conception of the community-Church, according to which the Church can hardly become fully responsible before the nation as a whole has been Christianized. This, incidentally, pushes the attainment of autonomy into some point in the indefinite future.

Warneck distinguishes three stages in the process of building a responsible Church. First there is the gathering of individual believers; secondly there is the forming of congregations out of these believers, and thirdly the joining of local congregations into a communion with an episcopal head. All this takes time, of course, and Warneck has been criticized as seeming to offer no practical theory of responsibility applicable to the Church in the foreseeable future. Even where self-government is concerned, he appears very conservative, regarding it as a matter of course that all local church-workers are to be subordinate to the missionaries, again, for an indefinite period. But, in all this, he is really trying to take the Church seriously as the Body of Christ and not just an earthly society. If he appears slow it is because he is profoundly concerned with the proper education of the Church. The question is, however, does he realize that the Agent in this education is Christ Himself? Warneck would probably have replied that he did just this, and that his concept of missionary education was therefore not just another form of missionary paternalism, but rather of expectant faith.

49

4

2. Bruno Gutmann

The Congregation and the Clan

In 1901, Bruno Gutmann, who was to exercise an important influence on the way in which the problem of the indigenous Church was to be treated in German missionary theory, was sent to East Africa by the Leipzig Mission. In an important series of publications, he deals with the subject of the indigenous Church, wholly from the standpoint of conditions in East Africa and from an anthropological point of view. He concentrates on the one question, how to use an indigenous structure for building a new Church, and writes with the conviction that man must be regarded not as an individual but as a member of an organic social unit. Man must be understood, he emphasizes, in, through and for the community. It follows from this, therefore, that, in the building of a responsible Church, it is essential to take account of the local community.

Uprooted from the community an individual convert is deprived of social relations essential to his full self-realization. Therefore, Gutmann argues, for the sake of the tribe and also for the sake of the Church, missionaries must not remain inactive while the traditional social institutions disintegrate. Still less should the missionary seek to destroy these institutions. Rather should he seek to relate them to the life of the growing Church. Gutmann fully realizes that the powerful ties of the clan often make it difficult for the individual to join the Church, but he urges that this difficulty should be borne, in the hope that ultimately not just an isolated individual or even a single family, but the whole clan or tribe may be converted. Only on such a basis, he believes, can the indigenous Church be built.

Gutmann is convinced that in all this he is speaking in the true Lutheran spirit. Only Luther's Church can send out missions, as he conceives them. He starts with Luther's doctrine that the Church rests on the Word, and interprets the Word as including not only Scripture but the power of God in creation, including human relations. So he concludes : 'Both the Church and fundamental human ties are created by God and are dependent upon each other and thus represent God's immanent Being in the world of men'. It is essential, if we are to do justice to Gutmann's teaching, that we recognize its theological basis which is strongly opposed to the policy of the pietists with their concentration on individual conversion and also to the teaching of some of the 'dialectical theologians' with their one-sided understanding of the Word of God.

Gutmann shows a genuine insight into the nature of the Church as a fellowship every bit as real as that of the tribe. He was concerned when as a young missionary he observed the disintegrating effects of colonialism upon the social structure of the Wadjagga people in Tanganyika. He was filled with respect and understanding, outstanding amongst missionaries, where the tribal life of the Bantu was concerned and, incidentally, made himself an abiding name as the authority on Wadjagga traditional customs. In all this he was concerned, not simply as a sociologist, but also as a theologian. He would have been horrified by the thought of a congregation which was little more than an audience to Sunday sermons, with less real fellowship among them than they had known before as a tribe or clan. Gutmann was rightly convinced that this could not have been the intention of Jesu nor the pattern of the early Church as we see it in Acts, and later missionary policy was indebted to him for his teaching.

This close association of natural ties with the life of the Church has some important implications for Mission. On the negative side, it means the abandonment of individual conversion except in so far as individuals, at the earliest stage of the mission, are considered the vanguard of the whole community. Further, if the community is the unit, it is virtually impossible to go beyond it; in other words, to go out in mission in an attempt to gain new members. Thus, Gutmann sees mission as the growth of Christ's purpose within the community. This is how he interprets the Kingdom of Heaven, as something present, existing for the community and among the members of the community in the attitude they assume towards one another. He is critical of eschatological presentation of the Kingdom in futurist terms.

On the positive side, however, Gutmann is rightly anxious to emphasize that it is the missionary's task in Africa to give indigenous social structures a new depth and significance by relating them to the Christian concepts of the Kingdom of Heaven, of man as a child of God and of our duty towards our neighbour. The missionary's task here is all the more urgent because, observes Gutmann, these ancient organic social structures are in a state of decay. They have no inner power to recreate themselves and yet they must be re-created for the sake of full and healthy human existence. The missionary it is who must revitalize them by transforming the tribal organism into a responsible Church. For this purpose the missionary must make the most responsible members of the community the pillars of the Christian communion. He must not, as so often, select the most subservient members for his assistants, men who will separate both themselves and him from the life of the community. On the contrary, he must seek contact with men who can permeate the old structure with Christian ideas by virtue of their natural responsibility and authority.

Gutmann put these principles into practice in his congregation in Tanganyika, making leaders of the social group *ipso facto* leaders and officers of the Church. Unfortunately, the result of this policy was that, when the German missionaries were expelled from Tanganyika after the First World War, there was not a single African pastor in the Kilimanjaro District, after thirty-five years' work. Even then, the missionary society was reluctant to appoint an African pastor 'because a holder of full spiritual powers, if ordained with undue haste, might easily disturb the structure of a responsible Christian community'. In fact, Gutmann was against the appointment of any African pastors hastily or otherwise, for the full-time work of preaching and pastoral oversight. Pastoral oversight, he believes, can be exercized only in co-operation with tribal authorities, within the Church. To ordain a man to the full-time ministry of the Word and Sacraments means 'sending him to the community' instead of allowing him, as it were, to grow out of the community.

There is obviously much muddled thinking here, as well as practice injurious to the growth of the responsible Church, mixed with a genuine and worthy desire to relate the Church to 'the main stream of the country's life'. In the end, Gutmann was compelled to admit the necessity to create a theologically well-trained African ministry. This, however, he considers the ultimate aim of the local Church's development, once more, a phenomenon of the indefinitely distant future.

Chapter 3

SUMMARY

WE have glanced at the views of six missionary thinkers whose writings have had great influence over the last 150 years. Each of these thinkers is also a man in close touch with the actual missionary situation, either through personal experience, or through intimate contact with those who have had such experience. All of them passionately champion the cause of the indigenous Church, and, although there are differences in their theological starting points, there are also many points of agreement in their teaching of missionary principles.

All of them, consciously or unconsciously, belong to the colonial era. This does not necessarily mean that they believe in all the political and economic aspirations of that era, but they are all influenced, naturally, by the climate of their times, though not all in the same way.

Venn, the Englishman, is concerned with creating in the colonies genuine responsible branches of the Church of England. As with enlightened colonial administrators, he believes that self-development is the way to self-determination, and it is his view that this process will take some time.

Anderson, the American, has no imperialist-colonialist aspirations, but he thinks, nevertheless, on colonial lines in so far as he represents, in the religious sphere, the Western, especially the American, optimistic expectation of progress through cultural expansion.

Warneck believes in the colonial 'mission' of the Europeans who, he thinks, are called to lead the coloured peoples out of their alleged cultural, economic and religious backwardness. These people, he believes, start with the handicap of all but ineradicable racial weakness, so that their only hope of progress lies in being led by the Europeans, especially Germans with their emphasis on good order and discipline.

Gutmann still belongs to the colonial era, but he has a more sensitive understanding of the native culture of colonial people and is sure that this must be preserved.

Allen is the least in sympathy with colonial attitudes. If he belongs to the colonial era it is as one impatient with it, on practical grounds, because of what he has seen in China—a reaction to colonialism which he believes will spread to all similar situations elsewhere—and, theologically, because he considers these attitudes a denial of the power of the Holy Spirit, at least where believers are concerned.

Davis represents enlightened colonialism, concerned to help the under-developed countries to advance economically and socially by their own strength. They need Western help—that is the 'colonialist' element in his outlook—but they need help to help themselves. The end of colonialism cannot be indefinitely delayed.

A second feature common to these six thinkers is the influence of their denominational tradition. Each one approaches the problem of the responsibility of the Church with presuppositions accepted, again consciously or unconsciously, from his own church-background. If this background is Episcopalian the likelihood is that the road to responsibility will be longer than if the background is Congregationalist, emphasizing the local rather than the regional Church. The Lutheran emphasis on correct doctrine, again, is likely to delay the achievement of autonomy on the part of the mission-churches. Nevertheless, to quote again Bishop Sundkler's phrase : 'transplantation involves mutation', and each of these missionary thinkers finds it necessary to modify his own preconceived denominational notions in the light of the missionary situation. So the Congregationalist Anderson is forced to make concessions to the Synodal or even Episcopal principle of church-government, and the Anglo-Catholic Allen so modifies his episcopal views in the light of his belief in the power of the Holy Spirit in the young Church that they come very close to Congregationalism.

On the whole, it is true to say that these six thinkers view the question of the Church's responsibility more from practical, missionary experience and considerations of what 'works' most beneficially and efficiently, than from what might in the narrow sense be termed 'purely biblical and theological considerations'. Even when they quote the New Testament, it is more with a view to understanding apostolic practice than to make known apostolic doctrine. Readers will doubtless judge for themselves whether

55

that approach is correct or not, and doubtless their decision will be determined largely by their own denominational tradition. A true understanding of apostolic practice, however, would certainly involve consideration of the apostles' faith, and the writers we have been considering, though not by any means indifferent to theological principles, certainly appear to give priority to missionary methods. It is impossible, however, to answer the question of the nature of the Church's autonomy (or, we might add, unity), without regard to the prior question of the nature of the Church itself. This is the fundamentally new angle from which the problem is approached today.

If these writers fail to make detailed theological examinations of the principles of missions, they are certainly influenced by theological as well as other considerations. Theological convictions are at any rate implied in their missionary teaching.

For the Anglo-Americans, for example, the basis of the Church is the Holy Spirit, given to the Church's members in conversion and baptism. It is the Holy Spirit who finds expression in a responsible Church, particularly in its three aspects of self-support, self-government and self-propagation. On this view, the independence of a mission Church is nothing but a proof that it has been adequately filled with the Holy Spirit. Church-autonomy is therefore a spiritual, and not a purely administrative, concept. In the German theory of missions, on the other hand, independence is not a spiritual concept. Warneck, we recall, argued that it was not 'necessary for salvation'.

We might say that, in place of the Anglo-American emphasis on the concept of church-autonomy, Warneck and his colleagues emphasize the need to relate the Church to the Nation and to Society. They feel the Anglo-American thinkers paid insufficient attention to man's natural social tendencies, as expressed in the ties of family, clan and nation. They themselves believed that there is a 'certain relationship between national, indigenous life and the Kingdom of Heaven'. Where the Anglo-Americans see the creativeness of the dynamic Spirit, the Germans see the mysterious working of man's social urges, given him by the Creator and manifest in natural ties and duties.

Yet, although there is a fundamental theological difference between these two general points of view, a difference we might

56

summarize as being between emphasis on God the Father-Creator and on God the Holy Spirit, there is a common link. This is found in the belief, common to both types of missionary theory, in the immanent divine activity in the Church. That is why the emphasis in both cases is on the power of God indwelling the Christian community. In both cases, too, it is the missionary who determines the reality of this divine indwelling of the Church and who, accordingly, assesses whether the young Church is mature, ready for autonomy. Since the young Church has to be mature in order to be autonomous, both theories of mission hold that, in order to be mature, young churches have to be trained, naturally by the missionary.

It is not only Warneck who stresses this need for training. Venn and Anderson do so too. The only difference is in their conception of the manner of the training. Allen is the most revolutionary of the thinkers we have been considering. He wants nothing but to develop fully the vital principle dwelling in the young Christian community, namely, the Holy Spirit. Again, the method of training is vastly different, but the need for training remains. It is Allen, Warneck's direct Anglo-American opposite, who writes a book on *Educational Principles and Missionary Methods* (1919), declaring in the preface: 'All missionary work is educational in its character and therefore educational theory should throw light on its practice'.

It is in line with this emphasis on training that the thinkers we are considering agree that the young Christians are to be regarded from the beginning as capable of sharing, according to their capacity, in responsibility for their Church. They are never so poor and so primitive that the missionary is to do everything himself, and they are not to be counted helpless because of their inability to carry responsibility which is inappropriate to their environment. It is a mistake, therefore, to try to build a mission Church modelled on Western patterns, with a ministry trained to reach Western standards and a budget of Western proportions. If the Church is capable of these standards, well and good, but these are not the essential standards by which responsibility is to be assessed. It is better to begin with a simple organization which can grow as its scope of activity is widened.

There is, however, this difference between the views of these thinkers : Venn and Warneck want the young Church to grow under the protection of an ecclesiastical organization whose ministers would be the missionaries, and into which the native Christians would gradually be incorporated; Anderson, Allen and Gutmann suggest that the missionaries should merely co-operate with the indigenous Church, which should be administratively independent of them. Neither group wants to see the native Christians forced prematurely to form an organization which they are as yet unable to support, hence none of the six authorities advocates a method based on expensive institutions. They all concentrate on conversion and the building up of local congregations. Venn's and Allen's formula, accepted by all, sets the limits of the activity of the new Church from the beginning.

There is, however, this important distinction. Whereas for Venn and Warneck, responsibility is an ultimate goal to be realized step by step, for Anderson, Allen and Gutmann the full responsibility of the local Church is realized at every one of its various stages of development.

One further point on which all these authorities are agreed is the common responsibility of all believers, corresponding, we may say, to the Protestant doctrine of the 'priesthood of all believers'. It would not be too great an exaggeration to say that on the mission field this principle of the sixteenth-century Reformers was rediscovered, or even put into practice for the first time. If one considers Davis's emphasis on Christian stewardship, or Gutmann's emphasis on the function of each member within the organism of the congregation, it does not seem over-bold to assert that, in Protestant mission-theory, the 'priesthood of all believers' is the basis of the responsibility of the Church, not only on the 'mission field' but everywhere. Similarly, though not even Venn, still less Warneck and Gutmann, expect the young Church to embark at once in organized missionary work on the Western pattern, all regard some form of self-propagation as vital from the start because, to them, Christian witness in word and deed is a basic condition of the growth of the Church, again not only on the mission field, but everywhere.

These missionary scholars, as we have seen, exhibit a considerable degree of agreement, but the agreement sometimes covers fundamental theological differences. Equally significant is their silence on certain questions which we today would probably demand to have answered. This means that any examination of their teaching will still leave open a number of important questions on missionary principles. What, for instance, is the connexion between the fact that a group of people felt the impact of the Gospel and were baptized and the missionary aim to build up an autonomous Church?

We receive the most diverse answers. Venn regards the initial group, in so far as they are true converts, as the shoot or germ of the future tree, containing all the possibilities for the future native Church. Warneck regards them as a kind of 'beginners' class', eager to learn. Allen, on the other hand, has unbounded confidence in the initial group, for the Holy Spirit acts within it and gives it the ability to begin its life as an autonomous Church. Gutmann has little to say on the importance of conversion, but believes the new Christians must, at any rate, have experienced that they are God's children so that they can reach a deeper understanding of their natural social relations.

If we proceed to ask 'What changes this first band of converts unmistakably into a Church?' we receive three different answers, which are occasionally combined. The first answer suggests that the group becomes a Church through a development in organization. The organization provides a link between the members of the Church. Anderson made this clear by using words like 'gather' and 'organize' for founding a Church. In this context, organization means both gathering the individual Christians into a local congregation, and gathering the local churches into a regional communion. Fundamentally, the six agree here. The second answer goes further than this, and would use the term 'Church' to include all the Christians in a given geographical area. Allen wholly repudiated such a 'geographical' conception of the Church.

Finally, some of these missionary scholars regard the ministry as essential for the Church, although they differ in their conception of the ministry. The Anglicans see this from the point of view of ecclesiastical law; it is episcopacy which endows a young Church with all its vital functions. Warneck, the Lutheran, regards the ordained pastor as the guarantor of doctrine based on Scripture and Creed. The third point of view with which even

Gutmann can agree, however critically he views the pastoral office, considers the ministry essential simply because the organism requires a leader. All these authorities leave open the question : 'Does the institution of a ministry transform a Christian "community" into a Church?' If it does, what is the minister's function? From whom does the minister derive his authority and what is his relation to the congregation? What is the nature of his 'responsibility' in relation to that of the Church as a whole?

The Church's responsibility, however, greatly exceeds the limits of organization for its own domestic life. Full responsibility will embrace such aspects of the Church's life as its relation to its environment, involving the difficult question of relation to indigenous culture and also the Church's relation to the State. It will also include the missionary task of the Church, not only in its own immediate environment, but also further afield, if not to 'the uttermost part of the earth'.

Was Anderson right, for instance, to encourage the young Church in Hawaii to send a mission to Micronesia, even though at that time (1847) Hawaii itself was not fully Christianized? Warneck did not mention the young Church's responsibility for evangelizing the outside world, and Gutmann rejected any such responsibility in what he considered the interests of an organic growth of the local Church. Then Davis revived and answered a missionary question which his countryman Anderson had rejected eighteen years earlier : 'What is the Church's social responsibility for the world? Does the exercise of this responsibility retard the spiritual building of the Church, or is this the way for the Church to fulfil its real purpose?'

Finally, there is the question, again beyond the mental horizons of most of these thinkers : 'What is the place of the self-governing mission-Church within the Universal Church?' The question of the organic, historical relation between the young Church and the Universal Church of past centuries does not exist, either for Anderson the Congregationalist, with his radically spiritual interpretation, or for Gutmann, with his radically sociological point of view.

If, however, we take seriously the organic connexion with the history of the Church, we find, in the main, three answers. The first is that given by the Anglicans, like Allen, for whom the only condition lacking in the Spirit-filled young Church (which only the parent Church can give it) is that of episcopal orders. The other two answers we meet combined in Warneck's writings. One is Lutheran : the historic continuity of the Church rests in its Creed. The other is biblical : the historic connexion with the early Church is the fact that the young Church is founded on the Word. We are, therefore, led to ask further : 'How does the young Church interpret its own character in the light of these answers, and what is the relation between these answers and the New Testament teaching about the Church's continuity?'

Most interesting is the ecumenical link between the young Church and the parent Church, formed by the foreign mission. What is the ecumenical function of missions? The six thinkers agree that the function of missions is a temporary one : it ends when the aim is achieved and an autonomous Church is created. They leave open, however, the question whether this function is only to found the Church, or to train it in full responsibility, and whether, in the latter case, such training should be authoritative or merely advisory? For the answer to these questions we shall have to seek the guidance of the New Testament on the ecumenical function of missions.

The last aspect of the ecumenical question, which none of the six thinkers attempts to answer, is the denominational one. Quite naïvely all these scholars tacitly assume that the mission-churches must conform to their own denominational pattern. Warneck is the only one who goes beyond this at times and speculates upon a possible union of various Protestant mission-churches in the future. This aspect of the problem reminds us that the autonomy of the young Church is limited by the obligations resulting from its being an historical Church and at the same time a member of the Universal Church. To this we shall return later.

PART TWO

THE PROBLEM IN THE HISTORY OF MISSIONS

Chapter 4

THE ANGLICAN CHURCH ON THE NIGER

On St. Peter's Day, 29th June, 1864, the first African—indeed the first non-European-Anglican priest, Samuel Adjai Crowther, was consecrated Bishop in Canterbury Cathedral. This was a direct result of Henry Venn's personal pleading. 'Samuel Adjai', he asked, 'will you deny me my last wish before I die?' It would seem also to be in direct conformity with Venn's policy for the building of a self-governing responsible Church. In fact, none of the conditions mentioned in Venn's famous statement of 1861 could be quoted in support of Crowther's consecration. The Church on the Niger had made little progress to self-support. No 'settled ecclesiastical system' had grown out of the Council system. In fact, the whole plan was an experiment devised at the mission-headquarters in London and was to create no small con-fusion on the field.

The story of Crowther's life is well-known : indeed, it is one of the most moving chapters in the history of modern Protestant missions, and Crowther himself, with all his faults, one of the most outstanding products of that enterprise. Sold into slavery as a boy, liberated when the slave-ship, in which he was a prisoner, was captured by a British naval vessel, he was taken with other released slaves to the freedmen's colony of Sierra Leone. In 1825 he was baptized, being given the name of a London Evangelical clergyman. He became the first student of the C.M.S. Teacher Training College at Fourah Bay, Freetown, and also visited England.

His abilities as a teacher and pioneer missionary were acknowl-edged as outstanding, and in 1841 he was invited to join the expedition sent out by the British Government to explore the course of the River Niger. Although this expedition met with disaster through sickness it had two permanent results. It showed that the Niger was navigable during the summer period, and that the tribes living on its banks were prepared to conclude commercial treaties. Moreover, the expedition led to a plan for a purely African mission to the Niger. Crowther's own part in the expedition was so distinguished that he was called to England where he received theological training and was ordained the first African minister of the C.M.S. in spite of the misgivings and opposition of many of the European missionaries in West Africa. He then joined the C.M.S. Mission to Nigeria and one of the first persons whom he baptized was his own mother, from whom he had been separated since his boyhood, and with whom he had become unexpectedly and dramatically re-united.

Venn entrusted Crowther with the task of founding the first mission-stations on the Niger, and when in 1857 Crowther was made head of the C.M.S. Niger Mission he was fully experienced, particularly in negotiating with local chiefs. He was also a skilful mediator between Nigeria and England, believing that it was part of England's duty to establish peace in Africa and to improve the lot of the people by giving them regular work, trade and social institutions. In spite of much disappointing experience of the effects of European trade and traders on the spiritual life of the country, Crowther continued to believe in the beneficial combination of trade and mission. 'Civilization advances' he said 'as Christian teaching prepares the way'. Some of his missionary helpers felt, with some justification, that he at any rate acted as if he believed that education and social and economic progress were more important than the conversion of the heathen, but there is no doubt that in his mind the two objectives were allied closely together.

In spite of staffing and other difficulties, the Niger Mission under Crowther made good progress. After another visit to England in 1863 Crowther was sent back by Venn with 'increased powers', and, the following year, as we have seen, he was consecrated bishop, again at Venn's instigation. Venn had long cherished the idea of the consecration of a native bishop, and in this he was encouraged by the C.M.S. Field Secretary in Lagos. Venn's own position is well expressed in his declaration :

'Missionary operations are essentially abnormal. The European minister is an exotic amidst native congregations and all attempts to regulate the relations between him and native clergymen have hitherto failed. The true remedy may be found in a native Bishop.'

The terms of Crowther's episcopal authorization made it clear that this was something less than the institution of a native diocesan episcopate. The Royal Licence declared :

'We authorise and empower you, the said Reverend Samuel Adjai Crowther, to be bishop of the United Church of England and Ireland, in the said countries of Western Africa beyond the limits of our dominions.'

That meant, as became obvious in the Archbishop's detailed instructions, that the new Bishop Crowther had no definite diocese, but was merely authorized to exercise episcopal functions in West Africa outside the British Protectorates. It is clear that an arrangement so lacking in precision as this one made by Venn and the Archbishop, with little or no consultation with the West Africa Mission, and, indeed, in the face of much local opposition, was bound to lead to friction and hurt feelings : it could scarcely be regarded as a move in the direction of the establishing of a responsible episcopal Church.

Crowther found himself placed outside the doors of a mission-area whose stations, with one small exception, were not under his jurisdiction, and it was left to the unwilling local missionaries to decide whether or not to submit to Crowther's authority. One of these missionaries, Hinderer, voted against Crowther on the interesting ground that the entire prestige of the mission in his area depended not on people's conviction that the Christian faith was true, but on their respect for the white man's superiority. The 'responsible Church' seems a very distant objective in such an atmosphere, and its realization was not helped by the manner in which the new bishop was consecrated.

Nevertheless, Crowther was able, with the help of his African assistants, to plant a series of churches along the Niger, so that within a single decade there were 600 baptized Christians, besides numerous adherents, under the care of ten ministers and fourteen teachers and catechists. The young Christians showed great steadfastness in resisting the influence of traditional animistic beliefs and customs, and some of them suffered martyrdom for their faith. Church-attendance was regular and there were frequent prayer-meetings. Moral standards were improved. Crowther writes :

> 'The converts have become industrious and more honest than their heathen companions, and the people in the oil markets regard them as honest in trade and prefer to deal with them.'

From the beginning of the Niger Mission, the most difficult question was where to find a sufficient and qualified 'native agency'. The workers in the mission were not 'natives' in the true sense of the term. Hardly one of them really came from the district to which he was assigned. Most of these African ministers and catechists came from Sierra Leone, and found the task of acclimatizing themselves physically and mentally, and of learning the local language, just as difficult as did the European workers. In general, their isolation meant a gruelling test which many of them found too difficult. Some fell to sexual and other moral temptations, while others, especially the high-school and college graduates, considered themselves 'wasted' in this unsophisticated environment, and showed a certain intellectual conceit which was not compensated by any real devotion to duty. In spite of all these difficulties, Crowther loved his workers like a father and had the reputation in the neighbouring mission-fields of having made exceptionally good progress in making his congregations autonomous. Yet, in actual fact, he did not try to realize many of Venn's original plans. His superior Sierra Leone workers stood socially almost as high above the local Christians as did the European missionaries; hence they were almost completely dependent on C.M.S. funds.

Yet the urge to spontaneous activity arose in all the larger local churches. Individuals voluntarily accompanied the paid workers on their preaching tours. In the Delta, preaching-stations came into being at which old pupils of mission-schools, or even a recently converted pagan priest, directed services and gathered together a sizeable congregation. Some of Crowther's European colleagues, however, showed more initiative than he in this respect and criticized his policy of employing the expensively trained Sierra Leone men.

A similar situation existed, closely related to this, in respect of Venn's first demand for self-support. Under Bishop Crowther, the Niger Mission cost the C.M.S. as much as or even more than its work in other fields under European missionaries. Local records suggest that administrative ability was not one of Crowther's outstanding gifts. Until 1878 none of the Niger con-gregations made a regular Sunday collection, and even then the change was due less to Crowther's initiative than to the example of the newly-constituted self-supporting pastorates in Lagos.

It would certainly appear that nothing was further from Crowther's mind than to found a mission-church which was to prove its indigenous African character in organization, dogma and ritual in opposition to the Church of England. Well did Roland Allen call him a C.M.S. mission agent in episcopal orders. The fact that the British and American churches were rich and generous in gifts of men and money, while the African Church was weak in these resources, seemed to Crowther a good and sufficient reason for opposing any nationalistic policy such as was beginning to be expressed in Africa at that time. Similarly, it was for him almost a rule of faith that all overseas branches of the Church of England should adopt the Book of Common Prayer, with the Archbishop of Can-terbury as their Primate. This, he said in a letter to the Bishop of London, is the surest means of safeguarding the unity of the Anglican Communion throughout the world. On the other hand, Crowther was passionately devoted to his own African continent and well understood the importance of preserving a genuinely indigenous heritage within the Church. There is no contradic-tion here : he believed Western civilization would raise the cultural, economic, social, and, above all, the religious standards of Africa. This view, however, was not shared by the new genera-tion which had absorbed the awakening spirit of African nationalism. They gave Crowther and his African colleagues the nickname 'Black Englishmen'. The African minister Henry Johnson was sensitive to this criticism and wrote, after a visit to Onitsha in 1877 : 'I hope we shall bear in mind the fact that the Christianity of Onitsha will grow weak and sickly, and that it will be devoid of all inherent vitality, if English be allowed to supersede the native tongue'.

It is not surprising that criticism of Crowther should have grown steadily, and that, in consequence, the C.M.S. should have tightened up the organization of the Niger Mission. By the year 1879, rumours about the spiritual situation in that Mission had become so frequent and so disturbing at C.M.S. headquarters in London that the Society arranged for an experienced missionary, Wood of the Yoruba Mission, to make a tour of inspection and to report. Wood's report confirmed many of the rumours and attributed the troubles largely to the fact that the workers in the Niger Mission were uprooted and isolated men, and also to the lack of self-government and self-support in the Mission. The experiment had shown that it was not enough to have a national Bishop; it was the Church which had to become fully indigenous and responsible. Crowther, however, though now over seventy and obviously too old for his heavy duties, was still held in great affection and esteem in London.

The series of half-measures with which the Society attempted to patch up the work of the Niger Mission did little good, and finally a European Mission Secretary, T. Phillips, was sent to the Niger as Crowther's adviser and as the local representative of the C.M.S., with wide administrative powers. Neither Phillips nor his three successors succeeded in reconciling these powers with those of the Bishop and the situation deteriorated.

Crowther himself grew increasingly sensitive to criticism, in spite of the great efforts made by the Society to spare him pain. As happens so frequently in the missionary situation, he took such criticism as inspired by anti-national sentiments, and his supporters incited the public to hostility towards the European missionaries. Crowther and his supporters began to clamour for complete independence of the C.M.S., though remaining within the Anglican Communion. It was hoped that the financial independence implied by this policy would be made possible by local giving, supplemented by support from Christians in Lagos and Sierra Leone, the Niger disaster having become a matter of national concern on the West Coast, involving non-Christians as well as Christians.

In the midst of the tragic confusion brought about by this bitter situation, Crowther died, on the 31st December, 1891. According to his doctor death was due to a partial paralytic stroke brought about by overwork and severe mental anxiety, but it was just as much due to the missionary policy of half-measures designed to conceal the logical consequences of an earlier policy which history had proved to be mistaken.

Samuel Adjai Crowther had been placed in an impossible position, as bishop, from the beginning; the wonder is that he achieved as much as he did. His son, Archdeacon Dandeson Crowther, in obedience to what he regarded as his father's will, constituted the 'Niger Delta Pastorate' and withdrew from all connexion with the C.M.S. The Society, on its part, wished the Christians of the Delta a sad farewell and suspended its grants as from 30th April, 1892. Crowther's successors in the Delta since have been Europeans, but his immediate successors, Hill and Tugwell, helped greatly to heal the wounds and to bring the Delta Pastorate back into fellowship with the Society.

Behind this whole tangled history stands the figure of Henry Venn, with his missionary principles. There is general acceptance of the soundness of the principles, but their application requires accurate timing, intimate personal knowledge of the local situation and the personalities involved, and, ideally, personal participation in the process. To attempt to apply the principles blindly must lead to tension, confusion and probable disaster. Venn once wrote to Anderson that he had learnt more and more to follow divine guidance instead of his own principles in missionary affairs, 'for principles which may apply to one Mission will often be inapplicable to a different field, as well as in different stages of advancement in the same field'. He regarded Crowther's consecration as 'a further step in the divine guidance of the Niger Mission', rather than as a clear example of the operation of his own missionary principles. So perhaps he was not altogether surprised by the later criticism of Crowther's mission-work as not putting these principles sufficiently into practice in the manner in which they had been applied in the Yoruba Mission.

But even if Crowther had carried out Venn's plans, exactly as was done in the Yoruba District, this would not necessarily have resulted in a mission-Church on the Anglican pattern. In the Yoruba District, what emerged was a number of self-supporting pastorates with very little connexion with one another. It is true that they were all under the authority of the same bishop, but they did not co-operate as a diocese until the time of Bishop Tugwell who introduced a full diocesan constitution for Western Equatorial Africa in 1906. Then only did the mission-Church of Nigeria have the Anglican organs of synod and diocesan board. In 1864, when Crowther was consecrated, the young West African Church simply did not have either the experience or the necessary ability for constructing an Anglican diocese. It would be unjust, therefore, to lay the whole blame on Bishop Crowther, unsuitable though he was for the episcopal office, as Venn understood it, on the mission-field.

Perhaps things would have turned out differently if Venn could have devoted his time to guiding his protegé and the local Church through the first difficult years, and if he had lived longer to support Crowther with his experience and advice. The Delta Pastorate adopted the diocesan order only in 1910, thanks to Tugwell's organizing ability, and it was not until 1930 that the Niger Church became completely integrated with the diocese of Western Equatorial Africa. From then on, a series of branches of church-work, which had so far remained unconnected, became integrated in one organization, and C.M.S. missionaries were again invited to help with the work in the Delta. As the old generation passed away (Dandeson Crowther died only in 1938) the mental and spiritual wounds of 1890-91 were finally healed.

A separate Anglican Province of West Africa, though proposed by Tugwell in 1906, did not come into being until 1944. It is sad to have to admit that Crowther's failure seriously retarded the whole development towards administrative autonomy in the West African Anglican Church, and no African diocesan bishop was appointed until 1951 when the constitution of the Province was drawn up, and then only in deference to African opinion.

Even now there is not complete provincial autonomy, as above the Province is the figure of the Archbishop of Canterbury. It is true that the Archbishop is appealed to only in disputes about the doctrine of the Church or if there is disagreement about the election of a bishop, but only when the Archbishop's jurisdiction is ended will there be complete autonomy in the Anglican Church in West Africa. Then only will Anglican Christians there, like those in other Anglican Provinces, be able to regard the Archbishop of Canterbury simply as the venerable Primate of the whole Anglican Communion, who is yet only first among equals, namely, his brother Archbishops. Then only will they feel the West African Province is truly, and in every sense, a responsible Church.

It is interesting to notice that the Anglican Church of Nigeria which, compared with some other mission-churches, has reached a high degree of autonomy, is not trying to dispense with the English missionaries, not even now that Nigeria has political independence. Occasionally one hears suggestions that a missionary is not necessary for a specialist, e.g. medical, post but that is due not to any prejudice against missionaries as persons, but to the fact that the Church is sufficiently responsible to be able to employ people for such posts, nationals or expatriates, on ordinary professional terms. The feeling is that a responsible Church and Christian community should not require self-denial on the part of the expatriate in order to meet its own needs. At the same time, present-day missionaries realize that there are important spheres in which they can serve the Church.

The C.M.S. claims that it is still guided by the missionary principles of Henry Venn, though in this 'post-colonial era' it conceives the 'regions beyond' no longer geographically but ideologically and functionally, as it proclaims the Gospel in those spheres of the nation's life which have not yet felt the full impact of the redemption offered to individuals and nations in Jesus Christ.

Chapter 5

THE EVOLUTION OF
THE LUTHERAN BATAK CHURCH

In the hilly districts of north-central Sumatra live the Batak, an agricultural people closely related to the Malays. Owing to the comparative inaccessibility of the country, they were able to pre-serve their peculiar character in race, civilization and religion until the second half of the nineteenth century when Dutch colonization and, in its train, Islam, penetrated the country from the south. Christian missions began with a small Dutch Free Church mission, followed in 1861 by the much more effective work of the German Rhenish Mission. The missionary historian, Julius Richter, goes so far as to call this German Batak Mission 'the crowning achievement of Protestant Missions in the Dutch East Indies'.

It is true that no other mission managed to evangelize a whole nation in the manner in which the Rhenish Mission did in Sumatra. The Mission set itself from the first to accomplish this task, turning its back on the old pietistic aim of converting indi-viduals, and, with this objective before him, the great pioneer missionary, Nommensen, proceeded to an all-out attack on animistic paganism. At first, he met with much opposition, especially from those who were seeking to preserve Batak inde-pendence, but this opposition collapsed after not more than fif-teen years, and then great masses accepted the Gospel. In 1879, 1,500 were baptized and the total community steadily grew— 21,779 in 1891, 103,528 in 1911, 368,535 in 1936 and more than 600,000 in 1956.

It is not to be wondered at that behind this mass-movement there should be a variety of motives and that sometimes the Christianizing process was superficial. Nommensen wrote in 1890 :

'People crowded in on me from all sides. They all clamour for teachers and missionaries who represent some kind of warrant of peace and prosperity. At any rate we proceed under God's guidance. The victory of the Kingdom of God is assured.'

Although aware of the danger inherent in the situation, with Christianity becoming 'fashionable', the 'vogue', or *masa,* Nommensen felt it necessary to make as rapid progress as possible, in view of the threat of Islam, and to leave to a later date the task of grounding converts more securely in the Christian faith. As the Mission progressed and brought peace, law and prosperity to the Christianized districts, more chiefs recognized Christianity as the salvation of their villages. It was impossible in this process to distinguish between religious and economic motives.

The Batak Mission at this stage has been called 'the typical example of the so-called Christianization of a nation'. It was characterized by a change from individual conversion to group baptism, and by a resolute attempt to Christianize social customs, particularly the unwritten code of law and custom known as the *adat.* The Batak's lives were regulated at every point by the *adat* which had been handed down unchanged from time immemorial. This laid down rules for all human relationships between relatives and tribal members, for the positions of chiefs and medicine men, the social protection of widows, orphans and strangers. The *adat* contained laws, any infringement of which was severely punished by the ancestors, regulating the economic and religious life of the village community. The Rhenish mission was forced to deal with the *adat,* if only because a code of civil law had to be laid down for the Christianized village community. The mission decided to preserve those parts of the *adat* which were not obviously anti-Christian. The result, although not entirely satisfactory to the missionaries, was that the social framework of the Batak community was preserved; this considerably facilitated mass conversions, especially in the Toba district. Soon enough the drawbacks of this method became clear; Christianity, as represented by the Batak Church, was felt to be merely a new law which did not presuppose inner conversion. Everything depended upon whether the missionaries could start in time with the necessary spiritual follow-up. The strategic principle of that period, however, made this hardly feasible.

The Batak Church was a good example of Allen's concept of the Church's 'spontaneous expansion'. This means primarily that the new religious community attracted the neighbouring pagans by its very existence. Freedom from the multifarious *taboos* which ruled and hampered their whole lives, release from the fear of evil spirits, the calm confidence with which their Christian fellow-countrymen suffered disease and death and, above all, the example of a new morality, had a strong effect upon the pagans.

In addition to this silent witness, the young Christians, from their baptism onwards, felt a strong urge to take part in active evangelism. In this they were encouraged by Nommensen, and some of the particularly zealous made evangelistic excursions on foot into untouched territory. The missionaries soon learnt to respect these evangelistic bands of young men who proved themselves not only equal to, but even superior to Europeans as pioneers. They were better acquainted with the country; they knew the native mind and native customs intimately; they were masters of the Batak language with its wealth of proverbs and vivid imagery. The pagan Batak were more easily convinced by the Gospel when it was brought to them by their own fellow-countrymen. This success led the Mission to challenge the whole Batak Church with responsibility for taking part in organized missionary work, and in 1899 the Batak Christians founded a missionary society (the *Kongsi Batak*) of their own for work in the pagan and Muslim districts.

The rapid spread of the Batak Mission might have led to a breakdown if the Church had not been strengthened from within. In 1866, two years after the start of the mass movement, Nommensen drew up a constitution for his new congregations. One of the most important features in this was the provision for the appointment of elders who were responsible for church-discipline, local church-organization and the administering of funds. These elders were not elected, however, but appointed by the missionaries. (As late as 1928 they were referred to as 'the ears and mouthpieces of the missionaries'.) In addition to the elders, who did their work on a voluntary basis, it proved necessary to create a staff of full-time well-trained 'native assistants' for pastoral work in the numerous branch-congregations. These assistants, who were given the ancient Hindu title *guru,* spiritual teacher, combined teaching in the village-school with conduct of church services and pastoral care of the congregation. They served also as a link between the missionary, later the pastor or *pandita,* and the elders.

This office of teacher-preacher was an ancient one in Indonesian society where the holy man was also a teacher of the people. In 1883 the missionary conference decided to train native pastors who would be in complete charge of village churches and administer the Sacraments. However, no attempt was made to follow slavishly the Western pattern of the ministry. The young men were not to receive full academic training, but were to prove their eligibility by practical service in the church. These were recruited from the ranks of the teachers and, as they had already proved their teaching ability, most of them made very satisfactory pastors.

How did the missionaries regard these Batak church-workers and officers? Certainly not as their equals. The missionaries' attitude is well summed up in J. Warneck's words :

'The development of the Batak mission has proved unmistakably that the native assistants in Sumatra, as probably in all mission fields among primitive peoples, cannot yet be left to form their own administration, much less to lead their Church. When a *guru* or a *pandita* has been left too long to his own devices, the result has almost always been disappointing. We do not doubt that Christianity will have a beneficial influence on the Batak character, at present so lacking in independence and initiative: only time will show whether this character will be changed fundamentally. The missionaries will need patience, persistence and understanding: they will gradually have to lay heavier burdens on the native Christians' shoulders in order to strengthen their endurance and sense of responsibility. On the other hand, the native Christians must not be treated like children.'

This is a significant summary : it reveals the three obstacles to the autonomy of the Batak Church. First, there is the Batak ministers' inability to take over the responsibility for the national church-organization. But inseparable from this is the European missionaries' belief in what Gustav Warneck, as we have seen, called the 'ineradicable weakness of racial character'. Warneck himself pointed to the third obstacle : the patriarchal methods of the missionaries who wanted to keep in their own hands all real authority in the Church, and particularly to initiate and control all the actions of the 'native assistants'.

Even though Gustav Warneck's own son Johannes clearly recognized this as a mistaken missionary principle he himself followed it in practice. This is revealed in his metaphor of a well-knit organism for the congregation : 'the assistants represent the limbs but the missionary must be the living heart which drives warm blood through all the limbs'. Here speaks the typical representative of a generation of missionaries who truly 'gave their bodies to be burned' in the service of the Kingdom and who were certainly not lacking in love of a paternalistic kind, but who were completely unable to see themselves as other than the centre of power in the body of the congregation. They justified themselves in this outlook by their conviction of the racial weakness of the people among whom they laboured, but time was to prove how mistaken they were, in no field more than in this Batak Mission.

For a considerable period the Batak Christians seem to have accepted the missionaries' opinion of them without serious question. They accepted, or at any rate acquiesced, in the Church Constitution drawn up by the Mission in 1881, according to which the Church, at all administrative levels,—in branch congregations, district pastorates or circles and regional synod—was dependent upon the missionaries. They even co-operated with the missionaries' policy and the Batak Church became one of the first to fulfil to a very large extent the demand for self-support. The Mission can certainly claim much credit for the encouragement it gave the Church in this development; the astonishing thing is that neither Church nor Mission should have concluded that a Church capable of such a degree of self-support was also capable of self-government.

The situation could obviously not continue indefinitely. It was intimately connected with the European colonial system, and when that system began to be challenged, as it was throughout Asia after Japan's defeat of Russia in 1905, the church-system came likewise under fire. Whereas the Batak had been respectful, almost servile in their attitude to their European *tuans* (masters), they now, in the early part of the present century, began to feel bitterly resentful against the 'European intruders'. In 1917 this movement of local patriotism led to the formation of the 'Batak League of Christians' (*Hatopan Kristen Batak* or H.K.B.) Under the clever leadership of the agitator, Hezekiel Manullang, this movement revealed itself gradually as an anti-European political movement.

The nationalist movement, which had originally been a secular one, finally penetrated the Church. It showed itself in various ways. The heathen national heritage of the Batak was revived and wrongly called an indigenous expression of Christianity. The ancient pagan festivals were held again and the old Batak gods invoked, while for everything there was a justification based on biblical precedents. The H.K.B. waged an unremitting war against the German mission, and, with the slogan 'The Batak Church for the Batak', demanded, understandably, a revision of the Constitution.

Though some of the Christians involved in this agitation still touchingly felt the need of the missionary's guiding hand, others attacked the missionaries with undisguised hostility and bitter recrimination, some of them matching words with deeds and organizing various independent, schismatic churches like the *Huria Christen Batak* (H.C.B.), now the *Huria Christen Indonesia* (H.C.I.). The missionaries belatedly realized that their traditional forms of church-leadership were no longer suitable to express the spirit and guarantee the unity of the young Church.

It had always been the policy of the Rhenish Mission to Sumatra to grant the indigenous Church autonomy, but this was to be a gradual process, related to the degree of maturity attained by the local Christians and shown in their willingness to take over responsibility. In the 1920s the Mission heads, yielding to pressure from within the Church, and forced to keep pace with political developments, began to revise the Church Constitution, giving the Batak Christians a greater share in Church administration (already secured in theory in the 1881 constitution but not observed in practice). Some of the missionaries, as Johannes Warneck wrote, greeted this development as both salutary and inevitable; others regarded it as pernicious, forced on them by irresponsible agitators regardless of the effect upon the Church.

The first tangible result of the new Constitution, finally adopted after long discussion and partly revised in 1930, was

79

that the Batak Church constituted itself a separate church-organization (the earlier schisms had given the signal). This new Church was called the *Huria Kristen Batak Protestant* (Protestant Christian Batak Church). The German mission committee gave up all power, and the missionaries themselves lost their supreme authority in all questions concerning the Church, local, regional and national. The Church recognition of the local chiefs also ceased, and with it (a loss this) the earlier stress on the unity of Church and nation. The chiefs themselves naturally felt embittered, but few of them had shown themselves fit for ecclesiastical responsibility.

Yet the new Constitution was far from satisfying those who demanded nothing less than a completely autonomous Church. The missionaries still retained a considerable degree of authority. They filled the highest offices in the Church like those of chairman and superintendents, for which it was difficult to find suitable Batak candidates. Moreover, the missionaries retained the right of veto in financial matters, and their right to supervise the whole school system (now complicated by the fact of government grants), the hospitals, pastors and teachers.

During the 1930s the demand for autonomy remained the gravest problem facing the Batak Mission. This problem was well summed up by Johannes Warneck in 1934, after he had been appointed Director of the Mission Board in Germany. He said :

'It needs courage to risk the step of granting autonomy to the young Church. We must trust that God can do His work not only through the missionaries but also through the weak and struggling Church. In spite of all her mistakes and lapses we must trust the young Church, must believe that the Holy Spirit will guide her. All kinds of events might occur which might force the missionaries to leave. In that case the Batak Christians must be ready to take the helm.'

Prophetic words, and the prophecy was to be fulfilled only six years later when war broke out between Germany and Holland and all the German missionaries and their families were interned. The years between were indeed eventful, with increasing responsibility steadily laid upon the Batak Church and the whole conception of the missionary's place in the Church undergoing a profound change.

Warneck claimed that he and his missionary colleagues would much rather have spent their lives on their primary missionary tasks, pioneer evangelism, pastoral care, training future church leaders, than in administration. Looking to the future he said :

'The missionary will remain the faithful guardian of the congregation, its adviser, comforter and conscience. He will be gladly received because of his spiritual qualities. He must resign himself to the thought that he is no longer the dominant figure in the Church's administration, and this will deepen the effect of his spiritual contribution'.

In view of these sentiments it may seem surprising that there should have continued to be violent clamour for church autonomy, leading to the outburst of pent-up emotions in 1940. Were the Batak missionaries in fact in agreement with their former colleague who was now their Board's Director? Or was the indigenous agitation for autonomy a nationalist movement, ignoring the real state of the Church and mission in that period?

The financial situation of the Batak Church during the inter-war years was complicated by relations with the Government, and this affected the Church's development towards autonomy. During the First World War the German missionaries were cut off from their mother country and this caused a serious crisis in the work of the Mission, in spite of the earlier efforts to make the Church, as far as possible, self-supporting.

After the war, the Dutch Colonial Government came to the rescue, and, in 1920, took the financial responsibility for the whole Indonesian budget of the Rhenish Mission. Though this was an almost miraculous help to the missionaries it was not without its drawbacks, and the Mission found itself greatly hampered by government regulations, especially in the work of the schools. The missionary society had to promise not to extend its work in Indonesia, nor in its other mission fields. That was salutary in-so-far as the mission could now devote itself to thorough rather than to extensive work, but the society felt hampered by its dependence on the Government. Not until 1930 did the Rhenish Mission regain full power of decision.

As we have seen, the pastoral work in the village congregations rested largely on the local teachers, and these teachers found themselves so overburdened with extra work in the now State-

81

aided and controlled schools that, as elsewhere, they began to press to be relieved of their pastoral duties. When, during the economic crisis of the 1920s and again in 1935, the Government closed many of the smaller schools, the Church was faced with a grave situation. It had to make energetic attempts to support the village congregations without the help of the Government-subsidized teachers, and also to rebuild the village school system itself.

The whole Church had to assist in this task and the Mission Church Council, therefore, decided in 1924 that 12 per cent of the congregations' annual income should regularly go to the central church treasury. In 1929 this contribution was increased to 25 per cent and this arrangement helped to strengthen the Bataks' loyalty to their national Church. Apart from the schools and village congregations, however, there were other responsibilities which came increasingly to be a charge on the central funds. These included the pastors' salaries, the cost of charitable institutions, publications, and the widespread evangelistic work which the heavily burdened central treasury found difficult to support.[1]

The missionary zeal of the Batak is praised almost beyond reason by the American observer, Merle Davis, who regarded the Batak as the Indonesian missionaries of the future, especially among the ever-increasing Muslim population. The question began to be raised with increasing force : were foreign missionaries still needed, and could a completely autonomous Church, such as the Batak Church was rapidly becoming, dispense altogether with the help of the foreign mission, even in the difficult situation of the period?

The 1930 Church Constitution was due for revision in 1940, and the nearer this year approached the more impatient became

---

[1] Some of these responsibilities were transferred to the almost dormant Home Missionary Society (*Kongsi Batak*) founded in 1899, which undertook by word and action to further the spread of the Gospel among the non-Christian Batak population, and to carry on some of the philanthropic work formerly the responsibility of the Rhenish Mission. This Society was extremely successful and its income by 1937 amounted to one-quarter of the Batak Church's annual budget. The *Kongsi Batak* had been re-organized and integrated into the Church by Johannes Warneck in 1921 and re-named *Zending Batak*, Batak Mission.

the Batak. At first it seemed as if the moderates would prevail, especially when the Synod's committee worked through the first draft of the new Constitution, in January, 1939, without making any sweeping changes except for demanding that the finances should be administered by Batak, and that Batak and Europeans should be equally eligible for all offices. Leading members of the Synod declared : 'This time the *tuan pandita* (missionaries) have granted us everything we could expect'. The Home Board, however, had serious misgivings about its missionaries becoming officials of the indigenous Church. They thought that this might well hinder the true autonomy of the Batak Church and also that from then on the missionaries would have to bear the blame for any mistakes the Batak made.

The problem of partnership between Mission and Church was by no means solved, and it was at this critical moment that the war broke out and, as we have seen, all the German missionaries were forthwith interned. Thus the Batak Church was suddenly deprived of its real leaders.

The three Dutch missionaries who were still in Sumatra took the initiative at this time and appealed to the 'Mission Consulate' in Batavia, which empowered them to take over the work of the Rhenish Mission, in collaboration with other Dutch missionaries.

The body thus formed, the so-called Batak Nias Mission, was recognized by the Dutch Government as the legal successor of the Rhenish Mission. Needless to say, this arrangement was not universally welcomed in the Batak Church, many of whose members felt that these Dutch missionaries had prevented them from winning complete independence which had seemed to be just within their grasp. A heated controversy ensued, especially at an extraordinary meeting of the Synod in July, 1940, and finally a compromise was reached, suggested by one of the Dutch missionaries. The foreign missionary was henceforth to be called *Kerk-visitator* (Church Visitor—very near to the present-day term 'Fraternal Worker'). His position was outlined as follows : 'He has free access to our meetings, houses and churches. He is always welcome'. That meant that he had no longer any official position in the Batak Church administration.

So, after nearly eighty years, the Rhenish Mission in that territory had come to an end, in the sense in which it had always been carried on. The young Church had finally separated from the parent Mission. But it was not an organic development such as the Rhenish Mission had hoped for; it was a violent wrench. There was a deep-seated lack of trust between the Church and the Mission, and only the future could show whether the young Church could really stand on its own feet and whether the breach could be healed.

For the present, the missionaries who, ironically enough, by their mission policy of building up a national Church, had called Batak national consciousness into being, were regarded as enemies. After the separation from the Mission, too, one of the immediate results was a revival of paganism, as in the period immediately after the First World War. Another result was the re-awakening of Batak tribal consciousness, leading to separatist tendencies in the various districts. It turned out that nationalism offered no firm foundation for the unity and autonomy of the Church : on the contrary, schisms were multiplied and the goal of a single, responsible Church receded. Then came the Japanese, and the Batak Church received its baptism of fire.

Although the Japanese occupation lasted only a few years, it was of lasting importance, both for Church and nation. The Church which, as we have seen, was apparently coming to terms with paganism, showed its inner spiritual strength as it was forced to come up against external pressure. It showed an increased concern for Bible-study, and everywhere both ministers and lay-men uncompromisingly rejected the Japanese attempts to impose the Shinto cult upon them. Indeed, new evangelistic activity was begun, especially by the 'Witnesses of Christ' (*Saksi ni Kristus*) Movement, founded by a pastor who was concerned about the impact of the Japanese propaganda on some of the weaker members of his congregation.

On the political side, the Japanese occupation gave the necessary impetus to the struggle which was ultimately to lead to the formation of the Republican Federation of Indonesia. In this struggle the Batak sided universally with national Indonesia and the Church had the closest connexion with the revolutionary movement. This, not surprisingly, led to certain problems. First, was the young Church strong enough to assert Christian character in a state which was 90 per cent Muslim, and at the same time to show complete national loyalty? Secondly, what was to be the Church's attitude to the Mission in this situation? (The political 'underground' movement resorted to terrorist methods in order to prevent the population from having any contact whatever with Europeans.)

The Batak Church showed much reserve towards the Mission and hesitated for a long time to readmit individual missionaries, owing to its sympathy with the more uncompromising nationalist elements. The Roman Catholic Church, it is interesting to note, continued to increase the strength of its European staff, especially for educational work, and made striking gains at this time, reckoning 23,000 converts in 1953 against only 8,632 for the Batak Protestant Church.

This state of affairs suggests that even a young Church, which has separated itself completely from the authority of the foreign Mission, is not entirely free in its decisions. The freedom essential to a truly responsible Church is more than just freedom from outside domination : it must also be inner freedom to be ruled by the Word of God, irrespective of the power of political and social climates.

The relation between Church and State in Indonesia is now changed through the formation of a Christian political party, largely in opposition to Muslim political influences, but it is doubtful whether this 'fusion of Church and party'[1] represents any really satisfactory solution of the age-old problem of Church and State.

The internal administration of the Church showed surprisingly little change. The Batak church-leaders, like their missionary predecessors, worked within the framework of the 1930 constitution, with its centralized organization under the Synod. In 1954, Dr. F. Birkeli, of the Lutheran World Federation, declared, after visiting the Batak Church : 'My main impression is that of a great living Church with active congregations and masses of Christians, but with all too few leaders'.

In 1950 there were only ninety pastors for a community of 540,000, with the result that each was more of a district or circle superintendent than a local shepherd 'calling his own sheep by name'. One consequence of this was that the local congregations

[1] Prof. Theodor Mueller-Krüger.

could have Holy Communion only about twice a year, but the Batak Church did not revise the Constitution to empower unordained workers like evangelists and teachers to administer the Sacraments. Even evangelists and teachers, and above all the teacher-evangelists, were in short supply, especially since the school-system had been nationalized under the Japanese occupation. So the Church was impelled to supplement the *gurus,* who did voluntary work in addition to their paid school work, by a new class of full-time paid church-workers, the so-called *porhangers.* These, though unordained, were fully trained as evangelists and were commissioned by the laying on of hands by the *Ephorus,* the Synod President.

Just as difficult was the problem of financial support. Important sources of income, such as Government subsidies for church-work and missionary salaries, were discontinued. As elsewhere, it proved easier to encourage local giving for local projects and workers than for more central responsibilities. Here, the unsatisfactory position of the pastors in relation to the local congregations was most apparent, and many of them were forced to look for subsidiary paid employment which naturally limited their freedom for church-work. A proposal to meet this situation by an increase in the 'church tax', levied on all members, was coldly received on the ground that this would mean a major change of custom and was therefore quite unthinkable!

It is of special interest to note two opposite tendencies working within the independent Church at this time. On the one hand, there was the wonderful activity and release of new spiritual power in movements like the *Saksi ni Kristus,* promoting the 'responsible selfhood of the Church' and, on the other hand, there was a marked tendency to become rigid, a complacent retreat to the position guaranteed by the established custom (*aturan*).

The most distressing feature of the Batak Church in this period was undoubtedly its isolation from the outside world, a heavy price indeed for independence. The Rhenish Missionary Society could do nothing, but other Lutheran bodies, notably the Tamil Lutheran Church of South India, offered to give fraternal help. Bishop J. Sandegren of that Church paid a memorable visit to the Batak Church in 1948 (in some ways it can be likened to the visit to Nigeria of Bishop Sumitra of the Church of South India in 1954, as indicating a new phase of Church inter-visitation). Pastor Tunggul Sihonbing also visited America and Europe in 1948, seeking ecumenical help for the Batak Church in its difficult economic position. He realized that the best thing for the Church was to join the Lutheran World Federation, and negotiations were started at a special meeting of the Federation in Trichinopoly, South India, in January, 1950.

The Federation required assurance that the Batak Church was, in fact, a Lutheran Church and the Church was given time to consider its doctrinal position. The Church found it difficult to understand the classic sixteenth century doctrinal statements of the Lutheran Church like the *Confessio Augustana,* with its references to groups like Anabaptists and Donatists, and finally took a step without precedent in the history of Protestant Missions.

Without European assistance, but with the help of other Batak theologians, the President drafted a new statement of faith which claimed to be both genuinely Batak and at the same time truly Lutheran. After this statement had been accepted by the General Synod of the Batak Church in 1951, it was sent to the Executive Committee of the Lutheran World Federation for examination. The new statement had the merit of simplicity so that every Batak could understand and use it. and furthermore it was stamped with the solid Bible knowledge which was one of the Rhenish Mission's greatest gifts to the Batak Church. With the approval of the statement by the Executive Committee, the Church left its isolation and was received into a world-wide federation of sister churches. At the same time, the Church was left free to maintain a position of complete spiritual self-determination, and, furthermore, was free to continue to have fellowship with other Indonesian Protestant churches with a view to bringing about an ecumenical union of Indonesian Protestant Christians.

In all this, the Rhenish Mission continued to feel a loving concern for her child in Sumatra who had outgrown her parental care, even though the Mission was prevented from giving practical expression to this concern. Pastor T. Sihonbing visited the German headquarters of the Mission in 1953 on his way back from the meeting of the International Missionary Council at Whitby, Ontario, and a consequence of this visit was the offer of a scholarship at Barmen for a Batak theological student, and also of a gift of hymn-books for the Church. The offer was gratefully accepted as a proof of Christian love, but the Church continued to be reserved on the question of missionary service. This reserve was due partly to nationalistic feelings and to the local concern to preserve church-autonomy. Also, like many other Asian Christians, the Batak, regarding themselves rightly as a Church, desired to have relations with other churches and not with missionary societies, which it associated with the bygone colonial era.

Pastor Sihonbing, in his visit to Germany, sought the strengthening of the relations between the German Evangelical Church, not simply the Rhenish Mission, and his own Church. With this objective made clear, however, the Batak Church expressed its willingness to co-operate more and more with the Mission and, indeed, manifested lasting gratitude to the Mission by naming its new University after the pioneer missionary Nommensen, called 'the Apostle of the Batak'.

The new connexion between the parent and daughter churches raised a number of questions for each of them. The parent Church had to ask itself what justification was there for the existence of a missionary society, and what was the society's position in the Church as a whole? The young Church, on its part, had to ask whether the desired partnership between Church and Church was really intended to be a 'partnership in obedience' to the common missionary task, or whether it was more interested in the independence it had achieved than in trying to evangelize Sumatra.

The ecumenical task of the Batak Church was not completed simply by joining the Lutheran World Federation. Representatives of the Church who attended the I.M.C. meeting at Tambaram in 1938 had been deeply impressed by the supra-denominational ties of the Christian Church manifest in that gathering. How could these ties be realized on the Batak Church's own ground? There was the problem of relations with the schismatic churches which had broken off from the main Batak body, one of them, the Indonesian Christian Protestant Church, with 70,000 members. The difficulties in the way of reunion with these groups was partly due to personal misunderstandings. Then there was the question of relations with the Methodist Church in the north, always delicate because of the lack of any comity agreement between the two bodies. Nationalist feelings continued to hinder the growth of closer relations with other Rhenish Mission communities and even caused the Church to lose interest in the Theological College at Jakarta—to which it owed its first graduate ministers—in favour of its own institution at Sipoholon.

While Batak nationalism hindered advance in ecumenical relations, Indonesian nationalism, which was just as powerful, had the opposite effect. Towards the end of the Indonesian struggle for freedom, the various Indonesian Protestant churches began to take an active interest in promoting an ecclesiastical union of all Protestant Christians, analogous to what was going on in the political sphere. The first step was the 1949 conference at Macassar which planned the formation of a National Council of Christian Churches of Indonesia. Although the President of the almost entirely indigenous Indonesian Conference declared that the Church ought to be characterized exclusively by spiritual union with Christ the Head of the Church, and not by nationalistic sentiments, the Conference itself adopted a markedly anti-European attitude, and, when the Council of Churches of Indonesia came into being in May, 1950, no European was given a place on it.

Was the emerging Church of Indonesia in danger of standing on a nationalistic basis instead of confessing Christ to the world? In view of this very real danger, the Batak Church's membership in a denominationally limited but world-wide communion, like the Lutheran World Federation, could not be regarded as a danger to the ecumenical movement in Indonesia, but rather as a very necessary corrective. The Batak Church may well be faced in the near future however with the need to decide whether it is prepared to sacrifice its own doctrinal basis, which unites it with all the member-churches of the Lutheran World Federation, or whether it will use its confessional maturity to give a firm theological framework to the future Church of Indonesia.

Chapter 6

THE EVOLUTION OF THE KOREAN
PRESBYTERIAN CHURCH

In the year 1890, an American Presbyterian missionary, John L. Nevius, visited Korea at the request of missionary colleagues there who had sought advice in basic methods of building a responsible Church. His visit lasted only a fortnight, but it was one of the most momentous in the whole history of missions. Five years earlier, Nevius had published an epoch-making book entitled *The Planting and Development of Missionary Churches*, and his methods, which gave concrete expression to the principles of Venn and Anderson, were largely responsible for the extraordinary success of Presbyterian Missions in Korea.

North American Missions, Methodist as well as Presbyterian, had entered Korea after the signing of the Treaty between America and Korea in 1882, taking Seoul as their centre. Before that date, and particularly before 1876, when the Japanese forced the Koreans to sign a trade and friendship treaty, Korea had been almost hermetically sealed from the outside world. This was a direct result of the policy of the great Yi dynasty which ruled the country from 1392 to 1910, and which sought by national isolation to preserve national culture and religion. The opening of the country to foreign influences led to a process of social change through a period of turmoil and suffering which reached its climax, though not its end, in the fratricidal wars of 1950-53 between North and South Korea.

At first, the two American Missions made pioneer journeys throughout the land, in order to acquaint themselves with the country and its people, and afterwards came to an agreement with each other, and with other missions which had meanwhile entered Korea, about the division of the country. The first two missions chose as their areas North-west Korea, with Piongiang as the centre, and Central Korea, south of Seoul. The rest of the country was evangelized by the Presbyterian and Methodist Churches of the Southern States of America, and the Australian and Canadian Presbyterians. The Northern Presbyterian Church was the largest group, and, by 1906, it maintained forty-six ordained missionaries and thirteen doctors. In that year their Korean Christians had not yet produced a single ordained pastor, but they had 140 unordained evangelists and nearly 200 teachers and Bible-women. There were 843 congregations with 56,943 members, although only 14,353 members were regular communicants.

From the beginning, the chief aim of these Presbyterian Missions was the founding of an indigenous Church. An early statement of the Mission Board of the American Presbyterian Church outlined the policy as follows :

'The aim of the Mission is to make the Lord Jesus Christ known to all men in the territory for which the Mission is responsible and to persuade them to become His disciples; to gather these disciples into a Church which shall be self-propagating, self-governing and self-supporting (note the order); to co-operate, so long as may be necessary, with this Church in the evangelization of Korea and adjacent countries and in bringing to bear on all human life the Spirit and principles of Christ.'

Two points in this statement are specially noteworthy. First, the autonomy of the Church is subordinate to the central aim of evangelism. There is no question of 'the euthanasia of the Mission' so long as this purpose is not completed. Secondly, evangelism does not consist merely in establishing contact between Christ and the individual soul, but ought to show its effect in the whole life of human society—a remarkably 'modern' conception of Mission. It was for guidance in carrying out this far-sighted policy that the missionaries sought the advice of their colleagues in China, resulting in Nevius' visit.

The 'Nevius method', to which, as we have noted, the success of Presbyterian Missions in Korea was largely due, has been summed up as follows :

1. Missionary personal evangelism through wide itineration.
2. Self-propagation, with every believer a teacher of someone and a learner from someone else better equipped than himself.

91

3. Self-government, with every group under its own chosen but unpaid leaders; circuits under their own paid helpers who will later
   give place to pastors; circuit meetings training the people for later
   district, provincial and national leadership.
4. Self-support, with all places of worship provided by the believers,
   each group as soon as founded beginning to pay towards the
   circuit-helper's salary; even schools to receive only a partial subsidy, and no pastors of single congregations to be provided for by
   foreign funds.
5. Systematic Bible-study for every believer under his group-leader
   and circuit-helper; and for every leader and helper in the Bible-
   classes conducted by the missionaries.
6. Strict discipline, enforced by biblical sanctions.
7. Co-operation and union with other bodies, or at least territorial
   division.
8. Non-interference in private law-suits or any such matters.
9. General helpfulness on the part of the missionaries, where possible,
   in the economic problems of the people.

Of these nine points, 4 and 5 are regarded as the most important by Nevius' disciples and, indeed, point 4 is usually emphasized as the most characteristic of his method. Nevius, like
Anglo-American missionary thinkers generally since the time of
Venn, realized that financial support might endanger and even
paralyse the young Church's growth, not only towards autonomy
but also to the full sense of responsibility for evangelism.

It would be wrong, however, to imagine that Nevius' concern
was chiefly an economic one. He sees the economic factor as an
aspect of the spiritual life of the young Church. The wrong kind
of mission-support, he says, is bound to lead to spiritual laxity
and 'rice Christians'. Therefore, against the old missionary policy
of providing every thing—church-buildings, salaries of full-time
ministers trained on Western lines etc.—he outlined his own
method which, from the economic point of view, amounts to
immediate self-support of the Church from the moment of its
inception.

Church-work during the initial stages is to cost virtually
nothing, apart from the missionary's salary. The first Christians
are not at once provided with a church-building and paid pastor.
They meet in the home of a member, and, when they become
too numerous for such domestic meetings, they will be able to

put up a small building for worship. Then, following St. Paul's example, the missionaries choose, from among the more advanced of the new converts, some who can exercise a certain amount of oversight, on a voluntary basis. The missionary will train them, especially in the conduct of worship, and, if the groups make sufficient progress, it will be possible to unite them in local churches and to appoint paid assistants, until finally the first native pastors can be ordained. These will replace the missionaries and make possible the organization of an autonomous and self-supporting Church.

There are, of course, certain obvious dangers in this system. The emphasis on self-support may not always be understood in relation to spiritual growth, but be related more to a spirit of independence and even self-importance. It might even lead to schism in the event of a misunderstanding between a self-supporting congregation and the supervising missionary or higher synod of the Church. Above all, opportunities for evangelism might be missed because a local Church could not find the necessary funds or personnel. Therefore, two strong links must connect the 'autonomous' Church and the wider Christian fellowship : the right of inspection by officers appointed by the whole Church, and the common adherence to the credal or other confessional basis of the denomination.

Only if the unity of church-order and doctrine is safeguarded can the principle of self-support be prevented from leading to the dissolution of the Church. Even this does not solve the problem of possible local inability or unwillingness to take advantage of special evangelistic opportunities, yet to break the general rule, even for this purpose, in one instance, is to render the whole system ineffective. If there was one local Church to which the rule was not applied, the others, it was felt, were bound to deluge the Mission with financial requests, and these not only for help in evangelistic work.

The Presbyterian missionaries in Korea believed that one of the surest means of promoting spiritual vitality in the Church was to give adequate Bible-teaching, not only to the leaders, but to all members. The Bible-class system, they maintained, is essential for the spiritual growth of a responsible Church. So, in Korea both missionaries and local Christians accepted the

93

Bible as a Book of authority, together with credal statements which could be applied by even the less well-qualified group-leaders and helpers.

The Korean Church is well-known for the prominent part which the Bible plays in its life. Two factors contributed to this. The Protestant missions, together with the great Bible Societies, from the start devoted themselves resolutely to Bible-translation and distribution, and the missionaries wisely decided to print the Bible in the older Korean script which was much easier to read than Chinese characters. Thus, there was soon hardly any illiteracy amongst Christians. The Bible translations and the literacy of the Christians made the vital Bible-class system practicable.

In 1890, the year in which Nevius visited Seoul, the Mission started its first Bible-class there with seven members. In the 1930s each of the 3,000 local congregations held an annual Bible-Study Course for which the members left their every-day occupations completely, generally for a week. The missionaries created a system by which the whole Korean Church, from the tiniest village congregation to the largest city Church, studied the Bible. For many, this system culminated in theological training for the ministry.

In a critical report on Nevius' method as applied to Korea, Roland Allen queries whether the fundamental principle was, in fact, self-support or the Bible-class. Allen tends to think these were quite separate features and goes on to argue, therefore, that even missionaries who do not accept the financial aspect of Nevius' method may nevertheless accept his emphasis on the Bible-class system. For Nevius, however, the two principles were inseparable. It is most unlikely, at any rate in Korea, that Nevius' method as a whole would have been so successful had it omitted either of them.

In continuation of the work of the Bible-classes the Mission opened in all its stations self-supporting Bible Institutes in which humble church-workers, men and women, 'exhorters', deacons, group-leaders, elders, assistants and Bible-women, could study for one or two months each winter, the whole course taking from five to six years. In 1936 there were 4,509 men and women studying in these Bible Institutes. This unique training has itself been supplemented, since 1917, by voluntary Bible Correspondence Courses.

In this way the Korean Church gained a whole army of lay assistants who shouldered the main burden of parish work and evangelism without over-burdening the Mission or the young Church financially, or forcing the Church to depend on the Government for subsidies. Only ordained ministers could administer the Sacraments, and after 1907 the number of these men grew rapidly. Their Bible-knowledge was thorough, and as a result they were gifted with spiritual insight and evangelistic zeal.

As the Korean Presbyterian missionaries, unlike their brethren in India and Africa, did not consider educational work very effective from an evangelistic point of view, they neglected this activity during the early years. Not until 1897 did the Mission begin to build up a simple parish school system to serve the young Church. This system of Christian elementary schools grew rapidly once it was started, and, to relieve the young Church of excessive financial burden, the Mission gave generous subsidies towards the cost. In 1912, however, the Mission Board discontinued these subsidies so that the whole burden fell upon the Church.

From the beginning of the Korean Mission, however, medical work played an important part. Especially during the early years it helped to gain official toleration for the Mission. 'The scalpel of the doctor was used to open up the land'—to quote the *Tambaram Report*. In 1901 the first mission hospital was opened, and during the years up to 1917 the other sixteen mission-stations were given their own hospitals, in accordance with mission policy. These, however, could not be kept open permanently because of shortage of staff and funds. The largest institution, Severence Union Medical College and Hospital, an American foundation, was opened as a joint enterprise of the three Protestant missions and the young churches which had sprung from them. In the administration of this institution the Korean churches were equal partners with the supporting missions, but the rest of the Christian medical work in Korea remained the branch of missionary activity least affected by Nevius' principles. In the rules and bye-laws of the Northern Presbyterian Mission it was provided that the hospitals should gradually be handed over to the Korean

Church, but, in fact, they were entirely managed by the missionaries until the 1930s.

Opposition to the integration of the medical mission into the Church came as much from the indigenous Christians as from the foreign missionaries. The Church argued that patients expected to be treated free of charge in Christian hospitals, so that large subsidies were needed from abroad. In fact, the Church received only 4,000 dollars towards the expenses of eight hospitals, while the annual income from patients' fees amounted to 300,000 dollars in a single year. One cannot resist the conclusion that the Korean Church did not recognize its responsibility for the ministry of healing, or it could quite easily have taken the small foreign subsidy on to its own budget.

Like all other churches of Calvinistic origin, the Presbyterians lay great stress on Church-Constitution, and they believe that the essential elements of their Church-organization are to be found in the New Testament. These elements consist, on the one hand, of the three offices of minister, ruling elder and deacon, and, on the other hand, of the synodal framework which consists, in general, of session, presbytery and General Assembly. These are all headed by a moderator, elected annually, who represents the whole Church. As the Presbyterian missionaries had come to Korea to organize 'a native Church holding the Reformed Faith and the Presbyterian form of government' the Korean Church followed exactly the Presbyterian pattern. We have already noted the procedure followed by the missionaries in organizing local congregations; these they then sought to bring together in a general body with a uniform constitution.

At first, the Mission itself provided the framework for this, but as the congregations, as well as the missionaries, increased in number, a united Council of Presbyterian Missions was formed. This was the ruling committee of the growing Korean Church until 1907 when the first all-Korean Presbytery of the Korean Presbyterian Church was formed, administratively independent of the Mission. The Moderator was a missionary and there were a further thirty-seven missionaries in the Presbytery, but the forty Korean elders represented a majority which grew year by year. When the General Assembly was constituted in 1912, the Korean Church had finally become a Presbyterian

Church on the Western model. Its outward growth kept pace with its organization, and the Tambaram Report of 1938 listed twenty-seven Presbyteries with about 350,000 members.

As Nevius' plan, from the beginning, laid great stress on self-support, the Korean Church early achieved a considerable measure of independence. On principle, the Korean Christians had to provide the salaries for their native church-workers, and this was possible only if the workers were extremely modest in their demands. The consequence was that the workers were not estranged from their fellow church-members by adopting a Western style of living. Similarly, as local congregations had to pay for their own church-buildings, these buildings were erected in a simple, indigenous, not Western, style. To a large extent, the Korean Church accomplished the two tasks of supporting its local workers and erecting and looking after church-buildings. After the formation of the first Presbytery in 1907, the young Church increasingly undertook responsibilities beyond the purely local level. Ten Departmental Boards were organized under the General Assembly, for mission, theological training, philanthropic work, and so on. The local churches gave 5 per cent of their income for these purposes.

How was the Korean Church able to shoulder these heavy financial responsibilities? Certainly not owing to unusual prosperity, for the Koreans have always been poorer than either the Chinese or the Japanese. It was possible only because of the sacrificial giving of its members. In 1927, for instance, every communicant gave 15 per cent of his annual income to the Church and even 'adherents' gave 5 per cent. Church-members were soundly trained in systematic giving, and, in 1930, a special 'Systematic Giving Board' was in fact added to the original ten Departmental Boards. 'Christian Stewardship' became one of the subjects regularly taught in the Bible Institutes and Classes, and would have made little progress without the work of those Classes. One might fairly say that it was the Bible-teaching that balanced the Church's budget. All this, be it noted, was many years before 'Christian Stewardship Campaigns' figured prominently in the life of Western churches. By 1937 the Church income had risen by 75 per cent—in seven years.

By now, the first aim of the Mission, to establish an

7

autonomous Church according to Venn's formula, had been established. Now arose the second question, how the foreign Mission was to co-operate with the Church.

After the Korean Presbyterian Church had been constituted, the United Council of Presbyterian Missions ceased to direct church-affairs, but remained as an independent advisory and auxiliary body. It mainly undertook special projects in the fields of literature, education and evangelism.

So that the Korean Church and the American missionary organization could co-operate more closely, a Church-Mission Conference was formed in 1954, consisting of the Korean members of the Presbyteries, plus all the missionaries. This Conference now has, in the main, the authority which the Mission used to have, especially in relation to educational, medical and other institutions. Since 1961 the Mission committee itself has been little more than the legal owner of mission-property and a means of strengthening missionary fellowship. Even this can hardly be considered the end of the process, any more than it has been in other lands.

This does not mean that the missionaries have no longer a part to play in the Korean Church. On the contrary, all ordained missionaries, like Korean ministers, are voting members of the Presbyteries and the General Assembly. Twice, in 1913 and 1916, the missionaries offered to resign from the Korean Synod, either immediately or gradually, but each time the suggestion was turned down. As Korean ministers outnumber them, the missionaries are not able to out-vote their Korean colleagues in these bodies, but their advice is eagerly sought and carefully considered. The missionaries are particularly welcomed as teachers, advisers and initiators of new projects. It has been well said of the Korean Church that 'it has found a way of utilizing its foreign missionary associates to the full without sacrificing its own autonomy'.

From the beginning, the urge to witness was a marked trait of the Korean Christians. The slogan : 'Each Christian teaches another person' was received by them with unexpected enthusiasm. The tradition was formed early that the candidate for baptism brought another candidate with him, as a sign of gratitude, when he was being baptized. The Korean Church had a very original method of stimulating this personal witness, called *naly-embo*, i.e., devotion of a number of days to evangelism. When, in a Bible-class, a local congregation or a whole district planned an evangelistic campaign, the members were invited to give up voluntarily a number of working days during the ensuing year for this purpose. This often led to an amusing competition among the members. Missionary work outside Korea was also begun, both amongst Koreans living abroad as well as non-Koreans. The Korean Church sent missionaries to a part of the Presbyterian Mission field in the Shantung Province of China and, when political changes there made it impossible to continue, they sent missionaries to Thailand.

Naturally, the spiritual life of the Korean Church has not developed evenly, in spite of some outstanding revival movements. As in other churches, there have been periods of decline and of renewed progress. The great revival of 1907, for example, followed a period when the spiritual life of the Korean Christians seemed shallow and in danger of stagnation. This revival played a very important part in the development of the spiritual character of the Korean Church.

The whole missionary staff in Korea had felt the desire to pray for a general revival among Korean Christians and concentrated their hopes on the large Bible-class for men which was to be held at Pyenyiang in 1907. 1,500 students came, far more than had been expected. Nothing unusual happened during the first days, but suddenly, on Monday, 14th January, 1907, the extraordinary occurred. A missionary conducting a prayer meeting asked two or three men to lead in prayer and in response the whole company broke out in audible prayer. 'Man after man', says a contemporary report, 'would rise, confess his sins, break down and weep and then throw himself to the floor, beating it with his fists in an agony of conviction'.

This emotional outburst started a movement which developed with increasing intensity during the days that followed and took the form of a revival of conscience. One after another began to talk with signs of profound despair about the sins he had committed, great and small, without fearing mockery or the penalty of the law, even of death. Everything was forgotten over the longing for God's forgiveness.

After the end of the Bible-class the students carried the revival into all the districts and local churches as far as Manchuria. The movement quickly grew beyond the initiative, control and even the approval of the missionaries, but the spiritual effects silenced all doubts. A widespread moral rebirth went through the Church. The visible result of the revival was a deeper spiritual insight and a great expansion of the Church.

Even better known than the 1907 revival was that which took place in 1909 and 1910 and which was called 'The Million Souls Movement'. This slogan, issued by the General Council of Churches, characterizes the most far-reaching revivalist campaign in the history of the Korean Church. It is estimated that during this campaign 100,000 'preaching days' were donated. Almost every Korean home was visited, 700,000 copies of the Gospel and a million tracts were distributed all over the country. Unfortunately, the result, expressed in figures, did not come up to expectations. The only positive effect seems to have been an inner strengthening of the Church itself, rather than expansion of the Church among the non-Christian people. One reason for this failure was very probably the national disaster in the conquest of Korea by Japan in 1910.

Even after the great revivals, the spiritual life of the Korean Church did not develop evenly. The ups and downs of the statistical curves clearly indicate periods of decline and of renewed progress. Political movements, in particular, cast their shadows from time to time. Nevertheless, periodically a 'Forward Movement Year' has been proclaimed in order to remind the Church of its missionary task and to strengthen its spirit of prayer and service.

The political movements, as elsewhere, have often made difficult the position of the foreign missionaries, and the Church itself had to face periods of hostility and even persecution, particularly under the Japanese rule. Some members of the Korean Church were actually involved in the independence movement of 1919, which the Japanese crushed with much severity. Many Christians were killed or imprisoned at that time, and in some places churches were destroyed and services suspended. When conditions improved, the part which some leading Christians had played in the national cause earned the Church a new popularity, but it cannot be said that the Church, as a whole, came up to the expectations of those active in the new political and social movements. Above all, the Church was unable to protect the people against the acute economic depression. The result was that many, especially the young people, lost touch with the Church.

There was further hardship for the Church when the Japanese military clique came to power in the early 1930s and, as in Java, an attempt was made to impose Shintoism on the people : 3,000 Christians were imprisoned and many were executed because of their refusal to deny their Lord, but lay Bible-students immediately replaced the ministers who had been arrested, and Christians took the Gospel to their fellow-Christians. The attention of all Korea was once more focused upon the Church. Unfortunately, in 1938 the Korean churches were compelled to resign from all ecumenical organizations; the war cut them off from the foreign missions. In July, 1945, a short time before their defeat, the Japanese induced all Korean denominations to join in one Church on the lines of the State-sponsored Church Union in Japan itself, the *Kyodan*.

Even the retreat of the Japanese troops did not mean liberation for the Korean Church. The section of the Church north of the 38th parallel underwent even worse persecution than ever, yet it did not break down, in spite of heavy losses. Now, the lay assistants had a chance to prove their worth. Wherever Christians gathered they prayed, sang, and studied the Bible, and erected little wooden churches, hardly more than sheds, to replace the churches that had been destroyed. Nor did the Church only fight for its own life. In this bitter period it realized more deeply its social duties towards the nation. It used all the energy at its disposal to save and restore distressed fellow-Koreans, whether Christians or non-Christians, in all manner of ways. President Syngman Rhee, a Christian, expressed his own appreciation of the significance of Christianity for the Korean people, when he said :

'Christian influence can be felt everywhere in this country : in the Government, in the National Assembly, in our country as a whole. Christianity gives a nation great strength, especially in times of distress.'

Mission remained the focus of the Church's social activity. The mission among the North Korean and Chinese prisoners of war was surprisingly successful. In the nine prison-camps, with 130,000 Korean and Chinese prisoners, there were 19,458 believers, of whom over 12,000 were recent converts. More than 10,000 prisoners attended Bible-classes held in the camps. In the cities the Church organized work among waifs and strays to save them from vagrancy and delinquency and, again, the emphasis was on Bible-study.

With this strong biblical emphasis, it might not seem surprising that the Presbyterian Church and Mission in Korea should have been conservative in its theological and denominational outlook. The Korean Secretary of the American Presbyterian Church acknowledged this not long ago, when he said : 'We began with an extremely conservative Mission and that emphasis was continued across the years'. Closely attached to its confessional statements on faith and order, the Mission's aim was the building of a single 'native Church holding the Reformed Faith and the Presbyterian form of Government'.

As early as 1905, however, the suggestion was made that, in the Korean mission-field, it was not possible or desirable always to be confined to the narrow limits of one's own denomination. So, at a joint devotional meeting of Methodist and Presbyterian missionaries held in Seoul, those present felt for the first time that the Holy Spirit was leading them towards some form of Church Union. In September of that year, the General Council of Protestant Evangelical Missions of Korea was founded, with the purpose, apart from the publication of a series of religious works, of 'the organization in Korea of but one Evangelical Church'.

Soon afterwards, however, these high hopes of union suffered a set-back through denominational loyalty. In 1907, the negotiations for union were adjourned indefinitely, so that the All-Korea Presbytery could be organized without hindrance. At the same time, the Presbyterian churches adopted a very definitely Presbyterian Confession of Faith and Form of Government, with a Book of Discipline, as a condition of its admission to the World's Pan-Presbyterian Alliance for which the Church applied later that year. The contemporary problem of the relation between Pan-Denominationalism and the Ecumenical Movement is suggested here. Needless to say, the Korean Christians themselves had as yet no say in the matter.

The Church Constitution made it clear that the Korean Church was absolutely independent and autonomous and could therefore decide later whether to preserve the denominational heritage of the parent Church, or renounce it in favour of a possible Church Union, but, in fact, this noble sentiment was quite impracticable. As in other places and traditions, a young Church, intended even before birth to be modelled closely on the parent Church, was bound to preserve the original form, at least for a considerable time.

The Constitution of the United Korean Methodist Church was the exact opposite. Its introductory doctrinal statement was nothing more than a statement of belief in the Lord Jesus Christ. It was evident that this contrast was going to render the attempts at a union between Presbyterians and Methodists difficult; nevertheless there was excellent comity among the six co-operating Presbyterian and Methodist Missions in the General Council. An important step forward was the formation, in 1927, of the National Christian Council.

The Church Union, introduced under Japanese pressure in 1945, was not to last for long. Against the wishes of the Korean Christians themselves, the American missionaries dissolved this on their return to the country after the war. The separatist tendency was further demonstrated by extreme right-wing fundamentalists who induced 250 Presbyterian local churches to leave the main body. The main body itself was not sufficiently tolerant to re-admit another group which had earlier separated over the Shinto question. The years of isolation during the war had not only strengthened the Koreans' power of resistance, but unfortunately had allowed a narrow spirit to permeate the Korean Church. This made it difficult for people to believe in the honesty and Christian faith of those who differed from them on points of doctrine.

The Korean Church had received a great heritage of confessional orthodoxy and Bible-study from its parent denomination. The ecumenical spirit based also on Christian love was perhaps a weaker strain. Well might the Koreans have complained, in the words of the South India laymen after the First World War :

'We find ourselves rendered weak and relatively impotent by our divisions which have been as it were imposed upon us from without.'

The Korean Presbyterian Church is now in three divisions over the not very indigenous issue of fundamentalism *versus* modernism. To bring these three bodies together again into one Presbyterian Church of Korea, and to bring that Church into organic union with the Methodist and Anglican Churches in Korea within the fellowship of the world-wide ecumenical movement, would be an achievement possible only through joint obedience to Christ in faith and love. Until that takes place, is it possible to speak of a truly responsible Church?

PART THREE

THE THEOLOGICAL PROBLEM
OF THE RESPONSIBLE CHURCH

Chapter 7

THE EVOLUTION OF THE CHURCH

It is a remarkable thing, and most significant for an understanding of the true nature of the Gospel, that the experience of conversion immediately leads to the desire to join a Christian fellowship. This has always been a phenomenon of the Christian religion, from the days of the Apostles until now. Johannes Warneck of the Batak Mission, dealing with the conversion of simple folk, said in his book *Life Giving Forces of the Gospel*: 'as soon as they are baptised, they form a communion'. This is particularly true of those with what is loosely called an 'animistic' background, because with them it is almost invariably the group, tribe, or even nation, and not just an isolated individual, which experiences the sense of liberation from the power of evil spirits.

On the basis of this missionary experience, we are justified in saying that the Church is part of the Gospel, an essential manifestation of the Gospel's power to redeem men in society. The Church cannot be built upon any other basis : secular education, medical help, rural and general social uplift may all be expressions of the loving concern of Christ, but they are not in themselves the foundation of the Church. By themselves they are but 'wood, hay, stubble' as far as the evolution of the Church is concerned, although this is a fact which has not always been recognized in the history of missions.

It is the Gospel itself which alone is able to break through the apparently impenetrable wall of tribal religion which encloses every department of life. It is the Gospel itself which reveals to men that the living Lord is the liberator, not only of the individual, but of the group. So we see in Nigeria, in the Batak territory, and in Korea, that the Gospel of Christ leads spontaneously to the desire for communion, based on the common experience of liberation by the same Lord, and this communion is strengthened by common loyalty to the Lord of all.

The main characteristic of this new communion is the converts' desire for union with God. This shows itself in the childlike manner of prayer. It was expressed also in the desire to be baptized and the willingness to attend preparation classes, in some cases over a number of years, as well as to observe certain ethical requirements which might very well run counter to the universally accepted customs of heathen society. Another striking characteristic is the spontaneous readiness to affirm their new faith in action.

In the Niger Delta, and still more in Sumatra and Korea, we hear of the young Christians' strong urge to witness, and this is complemented by their readiness to make sacrifices for the Faith. More significant than the fact that the missions in Sumatra and Korea expected their converts to support their own Church is the fact that the principle was so easily and willingly adopted. The Constitution of the Delta Pastorate proves that Crowther might have achieved similar results.

All this suggests that the three aims of Venn's and Anderson's formula are capable of being put into operation from the start. Witness, sacrifice and responsibility are not the results of a mission's policy of 'devolution'. They make such a policy feasible, but are, in fact, the spontaneous fruits of a living encounter with Christ as revealed in the missionary preaching. This contradicts any evolutionist theory of church-growth, as if the Church had to proceed from dependence to independence. As S. J. W. Clark acutely observed :

'Dependence is natural to the child, but it is not to the Church; the Church is often most virile in its infancy whilst the former is always feeblest then.'

It would be idle to pretend, of course, that this is the invariable result of missionary activity, but that is because not all missionary activity is truly the proclamation of the Gospel. Missionaries from the wealthier countries are easily tempted to use their, or their mission's, financial resources for social uplift, apart from the Gospel, especially when such action is greeted with enthusiasm by the local people who, like those of old, are only too eager to receive the loaves and fishes without the Kingdom. It is useless for the missionary in these circumstances to complain of his (sic) people's dependence, but it is not always easy for him to recognize that he himself has encouraged this dependence.

Our Lord's stern words to the 'missionaries' of his day who preached something other than the Kingdom of God, need to be in the minds of every missionary, whether from the West or from the 'younger churches', lest, like them, he enters not into the Kingdom himself and even prevents others from entering in. The greatest sin a missionary can commit is that of obscuring the nature of the Gospel in his zeal for 'results' and, through a conscious or even unconscious sense of self-importance, of encouraging a spirit of dependence which is foreign to both Gospel and Church.

With this word of caution in mind—it would be naïve to ignore its necessity—we may say that in each case we have examined we have found the early group of Christians forming a Christian communion with a degree of responsibility not generally expected until a much later stage of church-development. We have now to compare this phenomenon of missionary history with biblical evidence and the doctrines of the Church in order to answer the question : 'How and when does a Church evolve?'

No one who does not see the Old and New Testaments united in their message of God's saving purpose for all mankind can understand the New Testament conception of the Church. For the fulfilment of this purpose, God has from the beginning chosen, by His own sovereign free will, those who are to be the bearers of His promise to the nations. Not only has the New Testament idea of the Church its origins in the Old Testament; the very word used in the New Testament, *ecclesia*, corresponds to the Old Testament Hebrew term *q'hal*, and is used for that term in the Greek version of the Old Testament, the Septuagint. According to Dr L. Rost, the Hebrew term *q'hal* means 'summons to a meeting' and the purpose of the summons might be to gather men together for a religious celebration, a court session or a holy war.

The *q'hal* is God's summons to his people to gather together, and without this gathering together there is no effective answer to God's call. Similarly, in the New Testament the *ecclesia* is the People of God, the communion of those called to acknowledge Jesus as the Christ and, this is most important, called to acknowledge this together.

The Church is, at one and the same time, the community of the redeemed and the redeeming community. The Gospels emphasize that the Church is the present, visible form of the Kingdom of Heaven. It is both a spiritual and a social reality and, as such, corresponds to our Lord's own Person with its two natures. Any attempt, either in our doctrine of the Person of Christ or in our doctrine of the Church, to ignore one or other of these natures, contradicts the incarnational character of our religion. According to Christ's parables, the Church, as the form of the Kingdom, is already growing, in this present world; its full power is veiled and, we may say, corrupted by the sinfulness of its human members, but it is by no means invisible. On the contrary, in its members the Church is so unmistakably recognizable that mankind's salvation or damnation is decided by its belief or disbelief in the Church's claim to be divinely sent.

The New Testament knows nothing of any 'invisible Church' on this earth. The concept of the Church as a purely spiritual reality is the typically pietistic heresy. We saw its breakdown in the experiences of the pietistic missionaries during the mass movements in Sumatra. The New Testament conception of the Church is bound to include visibility because it envisages throughout the community of Jesus being given concrete tasks to be fulfilled in this world, in the midst of society. We might use a mathematical metaphor and say that the Church is three-dimensional : its height is its connexion with Christ, its depth the inner community of the brethren, and its breadth its relation to the world.

This shows the connexion between the New Testament teaching on the Church and the Old Testament idea of the *q'hal,* and also the difference between the two ideas. We saw that the Old Testament *q'hal* was a summons to a religious celebration, a court session or a holy war. In the New Testament the cultic sacrifice is replaced by the community gathering around the Word and the Sacrament; the court session based on law is replaced by the pastoral responsibility for one's brother, based on the Gospel, and the campaign or holy war is replaced by the mission which serves to extend God's dominion on the earth.

The new and decisive factor of the New Testament conception of the Church is the conviction that the summons issues from

Christ and refers to Him. Man's incorporation into the Body of Christ is the consequence of his experience of Christ : in the hearing of the Word, in response to Him in personal faith, and in the public confession of that faith in baptism. The constantly repeated illustration of this union in and with Christ is Holy Communion. In all this, man merely receives. The whole initiative is Christ's. The Church does not come into existence because human beings form a communion in order to come nearer to Christ; He calls the Church and as soon as it responds to His call the Church exists completely. 'Ye are complete in Him'.

The Church is a communion which has eternal life in its Lord. The New Testament makes no conditions as to numbers; two or three, gathered in Christ, are sufficient to constitute a Church, as Tertullian said. They can fulfil the priestly function of forgiving sins and, in this, they act as the priesthood of all believers. The New Testament does not claim that only certain authorized persons within the Church can call others into its fellowship. The Book of the Acts clearly shows that, in early Christian times, persons were baptized and local churches came into being with or without the help of the Apostles, although the Apostles remained ultimately responsible for the direction of the Church's mission. The actual missionary power of the Church was vested in the Word whose bearers, significantly were not expressly named. A Church exists wherever the Word is, that is, where Christ is active in preaching, sacrament and mission.

On this, the sixteenth-century reformers agree with the New Testament. The Lutheran *Confessio Augustana* declares forthrightly :

'The Church is the Communion of Saints in which the Gospel is rightly taught and the sacraments are rightly administered.'

Melanchthon adds to this statement the significant words :

'In this God works through the ministry of the Gospel and reclaims many for eternal life. In this Communion there are yet many who are not yet reborn but they agree about true doctrine.'

So Calvin :

'Wherever people listen reverently to the preaching of the Gospel and partake of the Sacrament, there, for that time, appears the Church manifestly and unmistakably.'

In this agreement between the reformers and the New Testament principles there is the decisive theological basis for an answer to the question about 'the responsible selfhood of the Church'. (1) A Church is constituted wherever people hear the Word and through it feel a need for the sacrament. (2) There can be no absolute autonomy in the Church, for the principle of the Church is not the will of its members, not even the will as disciplined and trained by Christian teaching, but the will of its Living Lord.

The concepts of self-government, autonomy, or independence, are, by their literal meaning and their political, social, and ethical analogy, unsuited to describe the nature of the Church unless they are given an entirely new content. Taken literally, they presuppose that the Church as a social entity can exist by itself, an impossible thing according to the Bible. The concepts can be used only in a particular and limited sense by which prefixes like 'auto'-, 'in'- and 'self'- refer only to human authorities and are alien to the nature of the Church.

Rule in the Church belongs to Christ, so that it is more correct to speak of 'Christonomy', the rule of Christ, in the Church, than of 'autonomy', self-rule. This, however, is not in any way to deny the importance of freedom from external human control in the Church, but it is to emphasize that that freedom is not the ultimate freedom. Luther's famous words on the freedom of the Christian man are apposite here : 'The Christian man is lord of all and the servant of none; the Christian man is the servant of all.'

Another interpretation would be to apply the prefixes 'self'- or 'auto'- to Christ as the true subject of the Church. But this confuses the issue which is concerned, in this discussion, with the responsible nature of the Church. Besides, there is the danger of implying a less than personal character in the relation between Christ and His Church. The same Lord who said : 'Ye have not chosen me but I have chosen you' also said : 'Henceforth I call you not servants but friends, for all things which I have heard of my Father have I declared unto you'.

Nevertheless, it is true that the Church is based on the saving acts of God in Christ, which alone make possible a free and personal relation between Christ and His people. As such, the Church cannot but be 'Christonomous', acknowledging Christ's rule of love as the principle of its life. This rule applies universally in the Church and there can be no 'autonomy' or financial 'independence' that discards it. So Bishop Sundkler, speaking of this problem in relation to the missionary situation, says:

'Even the youngest and smallest particle of a Church is, regarded from a Biblical point of view, a member of His Church, on the same level with other Churches and hence must be regarded by them as such.'

It might be objected that in this theological discussion we are getting a little detached from the real human situation. We are talking about the Church in the ideal or spiritual sense, when the only Church we know shows a very inadequate sense of Christ's rule or, indeed, of understanding of His Word. Are we at all justified in applying directly to the Church that exists in the world, especially in the under-developed and under-evangelized parts of the world, abstract principles that belong to the theological understanding of the Body of Christ? Conversely, ought not the question of responsibility in the Church be taken as a purely empirical and temporal problem? Should we not confine ourselves to the purely practical question of whether a particular group of Christians is or is not capable, not only of listening to the Word, but also of becoming living witnesses to this Word? To ask this, however, is to make an invalid distinction between the ideal and the actual Church, the invisible and the visible, and to confess failure to be able to receive guidance from the one for the other. Here again, the teaching of the sixteenth-century reformers is helpful.

Certainly, Calvin and Melanchthon would have repudiated too rigid a distinction between the visible and the invisible Church, the actual and the ideal. Calvin treats the visible Church with all seriousness, and provides it with a clearly defined constitution based on biblical principles. The same is probably true of Luther's teaching as a whole, though it must be admitted that, in some of the early writings, he lay greater stress on the inner aspect of the Church. Anxious to free himself from the Papal

8

Church, with its claim to be able to guarantee salvation, through its system of indulgences, penances and the like, Luther does speak at times as if he were concerned only with the 'religion of the heart'. Probably his inability to constitute a Church on this simple, internal principle led to his strange action in making the German princes heads of the churches in their territories.

Luther's acceptance of the principle that a man should follow the religion of his ruler (*cuius regio eius religio*) is notoriously difficult to reconcile with his principle of justification by faith alone (*sola fide*). We must probably admit that Luther fails to be consistent here. He sees clearly that the Word must encompass the earth, but he does not show quite so clearly that the Word needs agents. Yet, movements like that of the Anabaptists and 'spirituals', whose teaching Luther deplored, induced him not to stress exclusively the spiritual character of the Church. Hence the place he gives to the princes as secular guardians of the Church and, still more, to the ministry of the Word as a visible signpost, pointing away from the path to sectarianism and separatism.

The Church, then, according to Luther, consists of soul and body; it is both a spiritual and a social reality and both aspects of its life have their origin in God's revelation of Himself in Christ. The Holy Spirit descends upon the Church, calling it into communion with God, to be ruled by His Word, and the Church responds through the power of the same Spirit, in worship and in the confession of faith. Its dual nature is active in every part of the Church's life. The Church is a fellowship of human believers who are capable not only of belief but also of unbelief, of opposition as well as communion. Thus it is possible in missionary work that, although Christ has acted in creating a congregation of the faithful, the Church, in what may be called its 'responsible selfhood', has not yet appeared. The Church is truly in existence when, in response to God's call, His people exercise the three-fold ministry of worship, service and witness. And yet this ministry is not just a human affair which we can analyse and express in terms of secular psychology, sociology and principles of communication. It is essentially the activity of Christ made visible through His people, through human agents in an earthly situation.

For a proper understanding of the Church and of its mission it is essential to bear in mind its dual nature. God has called His people as labourers into His vineyard, but He and He alone is the Lord of the vineyard. His is the increase and the glory. The labourer's responsibility is a real one (I Corinthians 3.5-15) but the work is God's. This is particularly true of the missionary's task of building up a responsible Church. In all this aspect of missionary activity it is essential to acknowledge that God has acted and only He can guarantee the success of the work. As Dr. Johannes Dürr has said : 'That the Church—every church—belongs to God and is the property of Jesus Christ is the fundamental principle of the New Testament doctrine of the Church'. Where the messengers of Christ are active in church-building, gathering new Christians together in a visible, organized congregation with officials, constitutions and orders of worship, etc., (making clear, among other things, the connexion of the local congregation with the Church Universal) although the human agency may be indispensable, these human agents only acknowledge a reality which already exists in the mind of God, and which the thoughtful missionary can see coming into existence in the visible world.

Missionary activity is justified and fruitful only in so far as it is carried on in obedience to the Word of Christ which applies to every situation. The same is true of the new churches themselves. There is no autonomy which must be earned by human capabilities and resources like income, educational standards or social position which can then be proudly shown off; there is only the theological fact of Christonomy, the rule of Christ, inherent in the Church's nature from its inception. But, in order to prevent any pride derived from this divine freedom of the Church, it is warned by John the Seer that by disobedience this Christonomy can also be obscured and even lost. This is equivalent to the Church ceasing to be a Church at all (Revelation 3.16). This is not merely a social degradation, therefore, but a spiritual disaster.

If we compare this New Testament conception of the Church with some of the missionary principles relating to the Church current before the Second World War, we can only reject them as misinterpretations.

The Anglo-Americans were guilty of what we might call the

'vitalist' misinterpretation. For them, a Church could be made independent when it had shown satisfactory signs of its inner vitality. So they ignored the inner connexion between the Word who founds the Church and the effect of the Word in the new life of the Church. This life, instead of being regarded as a response to the divine call, becomes the state which the Church will reach when it has satisfied the various conditions set forth in the Mission's programme. Even if the Mission acknowledges that the life of the Church is a manifestation of the Holy Spirit, the situation is not greatly different, for the Holy Spirit in the Church is regarded as the property of the Church rather than as a continually renewed gift to the Church through the Word and Sacraments.

The conception of the Church outlined by the Whitby meeting of the International Missionary Council, as existing 'only by the Spirit' can very easily be understood in a manner opposed to the Reformation doctrine that the Church exists 'only by the Word'. It needs to be constantly reiterated that 'the Lord is the Spirit', and there can be no emancipation from the Lord, the Head of the Church, in obedience to Whom alone is freedom to be found.

In contrast to this, the conception of the relation between the Spirit and the Word, found in the Fourth Gospel, indicates that the Holy Spirit acts through man listening to the Word. 'If ye love me, keep my commandments, and I will pray the Father and he shall give you another Comforter, even the Spirit of Truth (John 14.15-17).

Roland Allen, the most consistent representative of the Anglo-American 'spiritual' conception of the Church, converts this relation into its exact opposite. He intentionally begins, not with the Word of Truth, but with the dynamic Spirit who gradually leads the Church to those experiences which correspond to orthodox doctrine. Hence Allen makes only guarded statements about anything connected with doctrine. This places him, in spite of his Anglo-Catholic principles, close to the tradition of the English spirituals like Barclay, who declared that it is the Christian life in the heart which makes a man a Christian, and that the Church is, therefore, to be regarded as a group of such men, united in their Christian experience. In fairness to Roland Allen, we must, however, acknowledge, as earlier, his sacramental doctrine which distinguishes him from those who hold a purely spiritual view of Christianity.

Allen's view that the indwelling Christ is immediately effective in the young Church, results in the work of the mission ceasing too soon to enable it to confront the Church with the Word which, said our Lord, is Truth (John 17.17). The mission cannot, because of a doctrine of the Spirit which is, to say the least, doubtful, abdicate its responsibility to declare the truth of the Gospel and to build up the young Church in that truth. Venn's view is not fundamentally different from Allen's here. According to him, the activity of the Spirit develops gradually, but in both cases it is sanctified man who constitutes the Church, rather than Christ's divine rule. It is possible to trace here Calvin's influence on the Church of England, particularly his view of the Church as a place of progressive sanctification. This view very easily degenerates into activism, as it not infrequently did amongst the pietists.

A very different point of view is what we may call the 'sociological' misinterpretation of the Church which we noticed in the missionary teaching of the German writer Gutmann. According to Gutmann the ground of the Church's unity is not the re-creating action of Christ in the Holy Spirit, but the existing traditional ties of race, soil and history which are to be preserved and renewed. That means, however, that the eschatological nature of the Church as a new creation is obscured. Our glance is directed not to the future, but backwards to the natural created order. But it is the Word which founds the Church, the Word which is the Gospel given through Christ, not the Law or, as we might say, the 'Word of creation', regarded in separation from the Gospel. In the Gospel, God's activity in creation and redemption are combined, but Gutmann seems to concentrate on the Word which establishes the natural order. The Gospel message is that the Gentiles should be fellow-heirs and partakers of the promise, not through their social systems, but in Jesus Christ. Hence, a critic of Gutmann's theory has pointed out that 'kinship obligations are of a legal nature, revolving around the idea of reciprocity rather than love, and are enforced by fear rather than by devotion'.

As a result of this sociological emphasis in Gutmann's theory of the structure of the congregation, the councils of elders ruled the people in a legalistic manner, and the influence of local custom had an equally retarding effect on the Batak Church. This socio-logical misinterpretation of the Church confuses Law and Gospel and regards both as expressions of God's creative will to save the world. Luther, it will be remembered, assigned to Law the nega-tive function of restraint, and regarded it as part of the old crea-tion which is passing away. It has no real place in the New Creation. And yet Luther himself used the idea of a national Church which must include a legal element.

The fact is that Luther's conception of the Church was on two different levels. Against the legally organized framework of the Roman Church, with its hierarchy of ecclesiastical authorities, he puts the priesthood of all believers. But, after the failure of his attempt to lay down a new Protestant Church constitution, he called in the help of the regional princes and justified his action by the medieval conception of the three 'estates'—ecclesiastical, political and domestic. He regarded them as orders of creation which find their fulfilment in the Church, and he therefore substituted them for the traditional priestly hierarchy of the Roman Church, although he did not claim that salvation flowed through them. But though Luther was right in considering the family and the State as servants and associates of the Church, he was wrong to place them on the same level as the ministry. This can only be regarded as a lamentable development of his earlier doctrine of the Church, and was bound to lead either to the Church's being dominated by the State—as it was—or to an alienation of the family from the Church.

Thus our excursion into the history of theology shows us clearly how the two misinterpretations of the Church contained in the writings of Anglo-American and German missionary thinkers are neither of them original to those thinkers. They are, rather, the results of ambiguities and obscurities in the Reformers' teaching.

Because the Reformers were unable to create a Church Con-stitution based solely on the New Testament, Luther had to bor-row elements from the medieval idea of Christendom, the one Christian Society; and the Calvinists tended to think of the Church in terms of a community of saints, separate from the world, a doctrine which received its extremest expression in the sects.

This lack of precision in the Protestant conception of the Church influenced missionary thinking in the nineteenth century, and affected missionary practice. Thus, our present difficulty over the nature of the responsible Church in the mission field is, at bottom, a theological difficulty and can be overcome only by means of a new and more truly Catholic doctrine of the Church.

What, then, is our positive conclusion from the New Testament conception of the Church? One thing which is clear is the right and duty of each congregation to proclaim the Word. Christ calls His Church into being and guarantees its existence by His presence in Word and Sacrament. The younger Church, therefore, no matter how young, must be entrusted unreservedly with the Word and Sacrament. These must not be limited to the occasional presence of a missionary : the young Christians have a responsibility themselves for the spread of the Word and for the administration of the Sacraments. The latter, of course, involves difficult questions of Order which would lie beyond the scope of our present enquiry; it is stimulating to note that these questions are being resolutely and responsibly considered today, especially in relation to the conception of a voluntary ministry.

In the period of mission history we have been for the most part considering, the challenge of this theological conviction was felt more vividly in relation to the ministry of the Word. In the development of the Batak and the Korean churches this was at least partly put into practice; in Crowther's missionary work it was in many cases spontaneously realized. And in none of these mission areas did this early introduction of native preachers lead to the spread of false doctrines. The missionary principles of Nommensen and Nevius agree in two important points : they both demand native collaboration from the beginning, and they call all members of the new Church to collaborate actively in the Church's mission to the world.

This affirmation of two New Testament demands amounts to a missionary re-discovery of the 'priesthood of all believers', a doctrine which, in recent missionary theology, has been more and more clearly recognized as the key to the problem of responsibility in the Church.

In the mission-field, this concept, which has so frequently been misinterpreted during Protestant history, regains its biblical meaning. In the mission-field, it becomes apparent that the 'priesthood of all believers' means, not primarily the rejection of the idea of a special ordained ministry or priesthood, but the expression in the life of the whole redeemed community of the sole priesthood of Christ. It is significant that this interpretation finds expression in every one of the recent schemes for Church Union—in North and South India, Ceylon and Nigeria.

It was an important missionary discovery, made by both Nommensen and Allen, that church-discipline is bound to remain ineffective as long as it is interpreted in a legalistic manner and, furthermore, restricted to the foreign missionary, instead of being exercised redemptively by the whole Church. This discovery deserves to be noticed and carefully considered by Western theologians: the priesthood of all believers, as expounded by Nommensen and Allen, is not to be confused with the self-assertiveness of Western humanism, but must be understood in terms of the Lordship of Christ and His call to His whole Church. All members of the Church, in obedience to their Lord, are workers together with Him in the proclamation and activity of the Word, both in the Church and in the world.

The degree of local co-operation in Nigeria, Sumatra and Korea differed considerably. In the Niger Delta the ministry remained voluntary and unofficial, at least during the pioneer period. The Batak Christians had a long and hard struggle before they were admitted to all forms of the Church's ministry instead of being regarded merely as the missionaries' 'hearing aids and speaking tubes'. The Korean elders and lay-officers were given real responsibility from the very beginning. This was partly because there were only forty ordained missionaries of the American Northern Presbyterian Church to preach the Gospel to a population of six or seven millions, and those missionaries were concentrated in eight stations.

We saw that the missionaries were not disappointed in their Korean assistants, largely because of the effect of the Bible-class system. In Nigeria, however, Crowther's greater reticence was caused by his continuing to regard the Western (i.e. Anglican) Church as his model, so that the responsibility of the local Church tended to be judged, as so often, by the Church's ability to satisfy Western conditions, which might or might not be appropriate or practicable in the local situation. It might have been entirely practicable, for example, in the England of Crowther's day, to provide a full-time priestly ministry in almost every parish, but to make such a provision an essential qualification for the existence of a responsible Church in the Niger Delta is a rule that might well be open to serious question.

Again, the German missionaries in the Batak country hesitated for three reasons : (1) They had what might be called a 'patriarchal' theory of the ministry, with all authority vested in the ordained leaders of the Church; (2) they tended to assume an attitude of racial superiority, not necessarily unkindly or superciliously, but just because they quite sincerely, even if mistakenly, believed the people to be not only culturally and spiritually backward—but also virtually incapable of spiritual progress. (3) they held a pietistic view of the Church as a gathering of 'visible saints', a view which might well have led them to expect spiritual standards and experience of a very high order, 'magnifying His strictness with a zeal He would not own'—a not uncommon failing among missionaries. Simple trust in Christ was replaced by the missionaries' ideal of self-reliance. Faith in the recreating power of the Gospel was replaced by educational requirements, and the biblical concept of sanctification was replaced by considerations of the human qualifications of the native Christians.

In all three points these missionaries deviated from the apostolic way of thinking and acting. Anderson and Allen emphasized that St. Paul did not entrust the spread of the Word to his young local churches because they were of a higher standard than modern converts in the younger churches, but because he was convinced that it is God Who makes the Church grow.

The mission-churches founded by St. Paul were even less dependent upon the Apostle for the administration of the Sacraments than they were for teaching. St. Paul himself refused to baptize, and we know that his converts observed the Lord's Supper in his absence. We do not hear of a special ministry for administering the Sacraments in that early period. In the Nigerian mission-stations this did not become at the beginning an acute problem. The Batak and Korean missionaries, however, both deprived their young Christians of the centre of Christian worship for twenty years by making the condition that they themselves must always be present when Holy Communion was to be celebrated.

There seem to have been three reasons for this policy of the Korean missionaries : experience in their churches at home had accustomed them to the idea that a full-time ministry was essential, and it was obvious that such a ministry could not be introduced at once in the mission field; they were afraid that immature, autocratic church-officials might cause a rift between Church and Mission, and they were actuated by the educational principle that they must train the young churches to appreciate the necessity for a full-time theologically-trained ministry.

There is, however, no New Testament foundation for the belief that the Western model of a minister, a representative of the general culture of his age, is indispensable. Above all, it is difficult to see why greater intellectual qualifications should be required of him who administers the Sacraments than of those whom the missionaries allow to preach. The danger that individuals might develop autocratic tendencies might have been lessened by authorizing a group of elders in the congregation to administer the Sacraments. In fact, this particular danger hardly ever arose. On the Niger, where Crowther dared to ordain humble catechists, these men, entrusted with such a responsible form of ministry, felt their own immaturity and the need for missionary guidance. The situation would have been similar in other fields if the assistants had been ordained. The educational principle as a stimulus for increased self-support certainly showed good results; but that does not justify the deviation from the New Testament conception of the Church.

From the standpoint of the New Testament, the doctrine of the 'priesthood of all believers' is entirely consistent with the need for clearly defined offices and functions within the Church. Although the New Testament teaches that all Christians are equal before God it does not claim that individual Christians may exercise all ecclesiastical functions equally. Instead, the Church is shown to be an organism in which its members have different spiritual gifts. It is significant that St. Paul mentions among these spiritual gifts (*charismata*) those which characterize the ministries or apostles, prophets, teachers and also administrators.

That means that these ministries are not incompatible with the priesthood of all believers, but are parts of it, functions of the priestly character of the whole Church. Those who exercise these functions within the Church (and it is important to remember that the lists given in I Corinthians 12.28ff and Ephesians 4.11 are of functions rather than of offices) are not separated from the whole body, but act on behalf of the whole body 'for the perfecting of the saints, for the work of the ministry, for the building up of the body of Christ'. The spiritual gifts they already possess are confirmed and strengthened by special ordination for exercise within the Church.

The ministry of certain members, duly called by God and ordained or otherwise appointed by the Church, renders the priesthood of the whole Body more effective. We must disagree with Gutmann's idea that the ministry of the pastor ought to be the final stage of the evolution of the Church. On the contrary, the ministry of preachers and pastors, which need not be bound up with Western methods and standards of training, ought to be among the first steps in the building up of a young Church. Hence the Mission must not wait until a ministry grows out of the Church towards the end of its development; the Mission, from the beginning, must hand on to the Church its own divine commission to proclaim the Word of God and to administer the Sacraments. The Church must have this ministry : it cannot function as a Church simply by the spontaneous activity of its members' spiritual gifts.

If the missionaries feel they should exercise the threefold Christian obedience in service, fellowship and witness, releasing the young Church from its obedience because of its immaturity, the energy set free by the Word and Sacrament cannot develop in the Church and accordingly withers away. This is the theological basis of the criticism levelled at Venn and the patriarchal missionary method. The three young churches we have studied all suffered such stagnation : the Church in the Ibo territory because Crowther failed to use the local people's urge to activity; the Korean Church because it dared not undertake its social responsibilities; the Batak Church because it relied on Government-subsidies for its teacher-catechists. In each case we saw that such stagnation threatens the young Church with collapse if the assistance is suddenly cut off.

Even more dangerous is another development in the wrong direction. This occurs if the young Church feels that the missionary claim to authority tries to withhold from it what rightly belongs to it as a Church. Under these circumstances the Church will sometimes begin to oppose the Mission, making vigorous demands or even taking by force what has been denied. It is particularly dangerous if what was first the opposition of certain individuals becomes caught up in a kindred secular movement, e.g., in a nationalist movement.

We saw in the development of the Niger Church and the Batak Church that this situation is fraught with danger because the missionaries believe it gives them all the more reason to resist what they consider an immature, unspiritual movement of independence. They overlook the fact that the opposition conceals a quite legitimate spiritual concern, namely, the young Church's knowledge of its direct relation to Christ, its autonomy in Christ. A nationalistic movement in a young Church is not a spiritual movement; it is a development in the wrong direction. But it is often a warning for the Mission to revise its authoritarian attitude to the young Church, and, remembering that Christ alone is Lord of the Church, penitently to become a servant.

If the Mission does not so react, various kinds of unfortunate results may follow. The Church may follow a policy of oppressive resistance. Nommensen noted this when he wrote :

'If we keep the congregations in dependence and do not initiate them into everything, they remain obstinate children who make our autocracy disagreeable to us.'

Or a schism may be caused between the young Church and the parent Church. Either some parts of the young Church form separate units, or the young Church, as a whole, cuts loose. A third possibility is that personal disagreements may receive a heightened religious significance if the Church or section which breaks off becomes entangled with the resurgence of local pagan religion. This usually renders the breach irreparable.

The South African sects of the Ethiopian and Zionist types are the best examples of this form of opposition in three stages. This shows that St. Augustine's distinction between a schismatic who sins against the Church's bond of love, and the heretic who offends against the unity of doctrine, often characterizes the way in which deviations arise and grow in the history of the Church.

There is no doubt that the young mission-churches, at the pioneering stage, often fell short of the ideal of the *ecclesia* as outlined in the New Testament. Fault may well be found with their spiritual understanding and their moral character. But Warneck tell us in his *Life-giving forces of the Gospel* that:

> 'the conversion of animists is usually not a single, complete experience but a continuous process through many years, beginning with the experience of the living God and culminating in a revelation of the forgiveness of sins: it takes the whole of his life gradually to understand the love of God and through it his own unworthiness.'

It is not surprising, therefore, that the young Church should exhibit a certain weakness in its earliest stage, but this weakness does not contradict its claim to be a Church. Some have suggested that the initial stage, when the Church is conscious of the living God, and consequently turns away from idol worship, is 'conversion to Law' rather than response to the Gospel, but the convert has this initial experience in and through the Saviour. It is the second generation which tends to treat Christianity as a code of Law, because it no longer accepts moral commandments within the context of the experience of salvation. This, however, represents not immaturity but degeneracy.

An intensive follow-up work is always necessary with second-generation Christians and their successors. The New Testament speaks of such churches, which have suffered spiritual reverses. The Church of Ephesus is threatened with the removal of its 'candlestick' (Revelation 2.5); that of Laodicea is threatened that Christ will spew it out of His mouth (Revelation 3.16). Yet the New Testament does not recognize any contrast between a dependent Church, an independent Church and a Church which is no longer independent. The contrast which is recognized is an absolute one: either the Church of God, or the 'synagogue of Satan' (Revelation 2.9). The Church is in existence from the beginning, when Christ brings the new believers together, but the Church is always liable to fall, and the missionary can rely on nothing to safeguard it from this fate, except the faith that 'He which hath begun a good work in you will finish it'. (Philippians 1.6).

As the young Church expands, its tasks increase. The collaboration of the local churches in a larger church-organization requires men with the gift of administration and the necessary experience. Neither of these is the automatic result of every conversion. Wherever, in the history of missions, the attempt has been made to proceed too quickly the result has been disaster. We saw this illustrated in the failure of Samuel Crowther, the gifted first African bishop of the Church Missionary Society. The cautious method of the German missionaries in Sumatra, and, to some extent, of the American Presbyterian missionaries in Korea, was in itself very wise.

As their Church develops it is the duty of the young Christians to grasp with their intellect the Word which they have already experienced in their conversion. They must understand Christian teaching more thoroughly because they themselves may have doubts, because they must try to convert their fellow-countrymen and because they may have to defend their faith against those who attack it. The growing Church has increasing social and political duties towards its nation and its Government, duties which require spiritual and intellectual maturity. The experience in Korea and in Sumatra, which shows that a young Church may be cut off from the Mission which carried out these duties for it, is a warning to take the need for this development seriously.

The Church is both created and preserved by the Word. That is why Crowther struggled up to the time of his death to translate the Bible into an Ibo dialect understood by all; the other two Missions similarly understood that the young Church could become mature only by becoming more and more firmly rooted in the Word. And yet there was a decisive difference between the Rhenish Mission-training for assistant preachers and the Korean system of Bible-classes.

Whereas in Sumatra, the missionaries remained firmly in charge of Scripture instruction, in Korea the young Church spontaneously became a community of Bible-students. Not until the 1920s, and later in the *Sakshi-ni-Kristus* (Witnesses for Christ) Movement, did the Batak Church develop anything similar. The secret of Nevius' system lay in recognizing and using the functional nature of the Word and of the Church. The Korean Christians studied the Word, not only in order to develop into maturer Christians, but also in order to be able to carry out their spiritual obligations towards others. The ministers, too, were bound to develop spiritually if their local Church grew spiritually. The young Church grew because of the Word; not because of some inherent spiritual faculty which developed through its own natural power.

Allen, who alleges that Nevius' system consists of self-support plus the Bible-class system, is refuted by the fact that the Korean Methodists, whose system included the Bible-class but not self-support, managed to surpass the Presbyterians in their readiness to give. The efficacy of Nevius' system depends on self-support through the Bible-class system.

When the Word of the living Christ strikes the Church or the individual Christian with peculiar and concentrated force, revival takes place. This is a sudden, living realization of the experience of sin and grace and, as such, is comparable with a man's first conversion. The revival presupposes that the rule of Christ is acknowledged. A revival cannot be engineered by a missionary or other evangelistic worker, for it is a direct work of the Holy Spirit, however much it may be prayed for and prepared for by human agents. This is borne out by the Presbyterian missionaries' abortive attempt to organize a revival movement in the Korean Church, the so-called 'Million Souls Movement'.

A revival is not necessarily a corporate movement; it can take place within the experience of an individual Christian, like his original conversion. A revival movement often causes a spiritual chain-reaction of more and more collective and individual revivals. Its importance is that it unmasks the unregenerate man who is hiding, as it were, within the membership of the Church and turns him to Christ who has died for the Church. Some of the results of meeting Christ afresh, as we saw particularly in the case of the Korean revival, are an increased interest in reading, hearing and proclaiming the Word and a greater fervency in prayer. Another striking result is an increased dependence on the Holy Communion, which Sundkler calls 'the Sacrament of the

Second Generation'. The young Church begins to grasp the importance of these 'essential marks of the Church' which do, in fact, constitute it a Church.

The contradiction between 'order' and 'movement' is apparent only. In reality, the movement safeguards the purity and steady development of the order. If a group of Christians relies solely on enthusiasm, they become a sect, dividing the body of Christ, or else, according to a well-known principle of sociology, their 'movement' settles down into a rigid framework, narrower and less flexible than if they had given due thought to questions of order in the first place.

The alleged decline from the 'spiritual' or charismatic order of St. Paul's earlier epistles to the 'institutional' order, (which many believe to characterize his later epistles) though frequently deplored by theologians and church historians, proves almost inevitable on the 'mission field'. It is, in fact, not decline but development. Those who speak of it as decline falsely believe that spirit and order are incompatible, or that, relying on the *charisma,* the spiritual gift, is the same as 'enthusiasm'. The fact that a Church, as we have noticed, can slacken in its urge to witness is very often an indication that that Church had identified the Gospel with a peculiar subjective experience. When the experience wore off the urge to witness faded. Brunner's well-known words : 'The Church exists by Mission as fire by burning' are true because the fire is the baptism of the Holy Spirit, descending upon the Church, and not some inner fervour related or perhaps unrelated to the Spirit.

The Church has been given the missionary task. The Batak and the Korean churches acknowledged this so completely that they felt compelled to create 'missions' of their own. Here we see the results of the wrong as well as of the right missionary policy. The Mission of the Batak Christians—*Kongsi Batak*—was a missionary society to which the Batak Church had delegated its own duty and in spite of that, or, perhaps for that very reason, the *Kongsi Batak* withered. Not until Warneck made it an integral part of the Church did it find new life. The Korean Board of Missions was definitely an integral part of the Church. According to the Church Constitution, all the local congregations were responsible for it. Here also, however, the spirit of giving lost its impetus, largely due to the institution of a church-tax which tended to make the church-member feel that when he had paid his 'due' he had done all he needed to do instead of being still an 'unprofitable servant'. What is needed is the living principle of Christian stewardship, which constantly confronts the Christian with his task and with the need for sacrifice.

The greatest danger to a young Church arises when the tendency to slacken threatens to obscure its vision of the true 'marks of the Church'. We saw, in the history of the Batak Church, that the formation of a tradition in a national Church can prevent the tendency to disintegrate, although it does not guarantee spiritual life. As we have already stated, the danger of slackening can be averted only by an ordered ecclesiastical ministry, not by purely 'charismatic' proclamation. There is great danger that this may be lost sight of in the (in many ways) commendable modern emphasis on the witness of the 'laity'.

Certainly the Church's witness must be of the whole *laos*, the whole people of God, but this is more likely to be enduring and effective if the Church is not just an amorphous mass of enthusiasts, but a Body with a framework in which there are many members, and one of those members is the ordained ministry. Both 'movement' and 'order' are related to Christ and His rule. A religious movement which is separated from Christ's rule destroys the Church's unity and weakens the very vitality which it thinks it is promoting; obedience separated from Christ becomes a cold and lifeless code. Thus spiritual liberty and church-order presuppose one another and remind each other that both are directed towards the living Christ.

During the early period of the growth of a young Church there are two dangers in its relation to the Mission. The Mission may create organization and institutions which represent burdens which it must carry by itself for some decades because the young Church is unable to do so. Or the Mission may forcibly prevent the young Church from undertaking its proper duties and thus drive it into opposition. As elsewhere, the German Mission in Sumatra exercised self-restraint in the matter of founding mission-institutions, whereas the Presbyterians in Korea, in spite of their good intentions, tended to burden the young Church with educational and medical institutions. With respect to church-

9

organization, however, the Presbyterian missionaries could serve as models to the Rhenish Mission and the C.M.S. There was never in Korea any struggle for the leading positions in a centralized missionary Church, for, since 1907 the organization has always been simple enough for Koreans to be eligible for all positions in the Church.

In Korea there were never any disputes about authority between missionaries and nationals : on the contrary, the purpose of Nevius' whole system was constantly to urge the local Christians to undertake more responsibility. At the same time, their experience with the tasks they had already undertaken constituted a salutary restraining element which prevented their tackling too much. The German missionary scholar Keysser's statement, that a young Church ought not to be forced by the foreign Mission into the framework of a ready-made church-constitution, but that it ought to grow organically, is borne out by this contrast between the Batak and the Niger Missions, on the one hand, and the Korean Mission on the other.

While weighing up the two dangers, an excessive burden, or an antagonism resulting from too light a responsibility, we find that it is one of the chief duties of the missionary founding a Church to discover the exact load of responsibility which the young Church can bear and to expect neither more nor less from it. Thus we can define the task of the missionary, as messenger from an older to a younger Church—as follows :

> The missionary helps the young Church and its members to find out what are their present responsibilities and, further, supports them in their discharge with the spiritual experience and material aid of his home Church. This calls for self-restraint in not keeping for himself responsibilities the Church may be expected to bear. There is no other way, for he may be called away at any time, and, even apart from this contingency, it is his duty to help in the building up of a responsible Church.

In this sense, one can agree with Venn's demand that the Mission should aim at 'euthanasia'; but this applies to any church-work which, according to the New Testament, should always point away from the agent and towards Christ, the real Initiator and Performer of every kind of church-work.

Persecution is the most extreme test for the young Church : it is forced to fulfil its task as a Church not only without any outside support, but against opposition which threatens its very existence. Persecution is a challenge which asks the young Church whether its true nature as a Church is worth more to it than peace, prosperity, property, life itself. The only alternatives are apostasy or martyrdom. This brings home to the Church its dependence on Christ and its indissoluble connexion with Him. St. Augustine found this vital principle of the Church even in the Old Testament. 'From the death of Abel to the end of time, the Church advances, wandering between persecutions from this world and God's comfort.' Luther, too, counts 'sanctification by the Holy Cross' (misfortune, persecution, temptation and evil) among the visible signs of the Church.

In two ways persecution is significant for the question of the responsible Church. Firstly, the foreign mission discovers that it cannot freely decide about its actions, or about carrying out its plans for building up a Church. Warneck's *gradatim, gradatim,* which envisages centuries of slow, gradual development, was written in the age of colonialism, in which the Europeans planned to train the Asian and African peoples gradually to achieve political and economic self-support, self-government, self-determination. The possibility of a radical breach with the West and its older churches, such as occurred in China, makes it clear that the creation of a Church and the granting of full responsibility to it must be one and the same thing.

Secondly, the persecution of the young Church makes it clear that church-responsibility must not be misunderstood as mere 'independence'. Korean and Batak Christians experienced in times of persecution the grief of religious isolation. That experience cures the young Church of any sense of inferiority or superiority, and enables it to assert its truly responsible nature without any strain. This is essentially St. Paul's attitude when he says : 'Not I, but Christ in me'.

Those who interpret the Church from the sociological and activist points of view see responsibility as the last stage of a process of development. To those who take the former standpoint, autonomy is the goal of the training given to the nationals by the missionaries. Those who hold a purely spiritual view of the

Church see responsibility as the final stage of an activist process which renders visible the Church invisible. The history of our three missionary churches proves that these conceptions are mistaken.

The Missions along the Niger and in Korea, which followed the principle of the three 'selves', discovered that these missionary aims could be achieved at the beginning as well as at the end. The Church Missionary Society, when introducing the principle of self-support in the Niger Delta, realized that financial independence is not necessarily the expression of a corresponding degree of spiritual maturity. In Korea it became apparent that maturity was reached, not by developing the spiritual life from the tiny seed by means of self-support, but by the daily use of the Bible. In Nigeria and Korea the Church did not finally become separate from the Mission but both churches demanded further intensive collaboration on the part of the missionaries.

Contrary to the views of those who looked for the formation of a national Church (*Volkskirche*), in none of these missionary churches did the national framework prove strong enough, not even in the Batak Mission where the Church had been purposely constructed on these lines. The process of missionary education, begun in accordance with this sociological view of the Church, led in the Batak Church to the explosion of 1940. The Batak Mission, like the two others, did not arrive at the final stage of the complete independence of the 'national Church' from the Western Church which Gustav Warneck had outlined.

On the other hand, we observed in the histories of the three young churches three points which they had in common. The reality of the Church which is truly under Christ's rule appeared in each case at the inception of the Christian community. Yet, in each case, an inner growth of religious understanding and evangelistic outreach proved necessary and practicable. As far as we can judge today, each of these three young churches tries to strengthen and deepen its connexion with its parent Church.

The process of development in the three churches was neither sociological nor activist. It was a development towards full responsibility, but its watchword was the divine paradox, 'Grow to become what you are'. The initial rule of Christ, which appeared in the first signs of life in the young Church, had to prove itself in obedience during the ensuing struggles and amidst ever-increasing duties. Although one result of this struggle, with its ups and downs, was that the framework of the Church became unmistakably firmer, the Church cannot be defined except by the concept used already for the initial stage, although its organization and understanding were developing more and more 'in Christ'. This reflects the New Testament conception of the Church which has been defined as 'the self-realization of the Lord and Saviour'.

The Church can live only if the branch is attached to the vine. Hence, there can be no purely independent existence of the Church, not even in its capacity as His Body. This has nothing to do with the humanist idea of self-realization. The New Testament frequently mentions the necessity of growth; but if one analyses the passages in question one finds that they do not apply to the 'faithful', but to the Word of Christ Himself who is to grow in them (cf. John 3.30). The growth of the Church is not some human thing added to the rule of Christ which is already in existence; it is an indispensable sign of the rule of Christ. As Calvin said :

'God works on her daily to smooth out the wrinkles and remove the blemishes. For this is the sanctity of the Church, that she progresses daily but is not yet perfect. Daily she takes a step forward but has not yet reached the goal of sanctity.'

Thus the truly responsible nature of the Church and the development towards it are nothing but an expression in the life of the Church of the relation between justification and sanctification. A theology of Mission which sees the declaration of responsibility as the end of a process of development is guilty of teaching 'justification by works'. The one foundation of the Church is Christ's unique act of redemption which we must try again and again to comprehend through faith.

In the New Testament doctrine of holiness the whole emphasis is on freedom, not on form. But because of its eschatological nature, because the Church has its ultimate origin 'from above', and not from any merely human association, the Church can become what it is, the community of the redeemed, only by the constantly renewed power of the Holy Spirit. In this present age the task of the Church is infinite, but that is precisely why Kraemer declares :

> 'Full selfhood is essential for the life of the Church. If you want to wait till you have achieved complete maturity you will have to wait till the end of time.'

Once more we ask critically : does this apply only to faith, or to missionary action as well? Our whole conception would break down if we were to separate the inner from the external Church, i.e., if what has been evolved here were applicable only to the invisible Church, but not to the young churches of Asia and Africa. The New Testament and the Reformers are far from this realm of thought, which has a closer connexion with Platonism than with the Bible. Nor must we distinguish between a communion of faith and an organized Church : the Church is not only obliged to create for itself an organization for the task of ministering to the world, but itself is essentially a ministry of the Word. That is why the rule of Christ in it, founded on justification, creates, from the beginning, the ministry in the Church.

This ministry is not a twenty-first birthday present from the Mission to the young Church which has been declared mature, autonomous, but is an integral part of the commission given by Christ to His Church. Thus, the responsible nature of the Church means that its external aspect, its ministry and the authority attached to it, grow as well as its inner communion with Christ. Thus the Church, inwardly and outwardly, is called to 'responsible selfhood' to the end of time.

Chapter 8

THE RESPONSIBLE NATURE OF THE CHURCH
IN RELATION TO ITS ENVIRONMENT

WHEN we consider the responsible nature of the Church in relation to its environment, the problem we have been discussing so
far assumes new aspects. In the first place, we see the need for
the Church to be truly representative of the community in which
it is placed in this world. It is the Body of Christ, no doubt, but
not some phantom body such as certain early heretics ascribed
to our Lord. It is the New Creation in Christ, closely related to
the bodily conditions, the physical, cultural and political circumstances of the country in which it has its visible existence. As
such, the young Church must assert its own indigenous character
over against the parent Church. Secondly, it must assert its nature
as the local embodiment of Christ's Church in communion with
the Church Universal and therefore in contrast to its environment. In theological language, the Church must maintain its
eschatological character as distinct from all human, social and
cultural forms.

That the Church is a stranger in this world was made obvious
by the fact that missionaries went overseas to proclaim the
Gospel under conditions unfamiliar to them. This was true of
the very earliest missionary activity of the Church in New Testament times; it is also clearly apparent in the modern missionary
enterprise. Thus, even the African church-workers who went to
the Niger from Sierra Leone encountered a large number of
climatic, geographical, linguistic, ethnological and sociological
problems which brought it home to them and to others that they
were strangers.

The churches in Sumatra and in Korea could never have become 'national churches' in a Christian sense had not the German
and American missionaries done their best to adapt themselves to
the national character and tradition; and yet the Germans could

not become Batak, nor the Americans Koreans, any more than the Sierra Leonians could become Ibo. But, where external circumstances limited the missionaries' renunciation of their European character, the love which they showed in their missionary devotion to a large extent bridged the gulf. However, the missionary situation in the three churches discussed made it evident that Christian nationals had to become the main agents of the Church. This tension between the national and supranational character of the Church is harmful only when it is expressed in a situation created by unspiritual factors like personal rivalry, ambition and resentment. As an expression of the 'two-nature' character of the Church, as in some sense an 'extension of the Incarnation', it is not harmful but creative.

Since the Shanghai Missionary Conference in 1922, the point most strongly emphasized in discussions of this problem has been the foreignness of the Western churches themselves, rather than of their missionary representatives. It is claimed that these churches, in their organization, liturgy and even theological approach, have adopted an historic form which is bound to remain inaccessible to Asians and Africans. It is a striking fact that this problem does not seem to have affected the spread and adoption of the Gospel on the Niger, in Sumatra or in Korea in any material way. The message of the missionaries was understood by the people, and, on the basis of that message, the Church was created. That was the essential thing, and Western forms were adopted as the expression of the new religion.

Until the pagan renaissance in the Batak territory, we never hear of any Batak opposition to the Western ecclesiastical forms of the Batak mission Church. Nor were such objections raised in Korea. This fact is a warning against over-estimating the importance of the problem of 'indigenization'. One cannot help suspecting that those who over-stress the point regard the Church mainly as a natural or social institution. 'But in that case', says the German missionary thinker Holsten, 'the vital question is the mutual influence of the Church and other social units, and the importance of the individual's social background for his conversion and the strengthening of his faith'. Our assumption is confirmed by the fact that, in the typically Anglo-American view of missions, which emphasizes the spiritual nature of the Church as, for example, in the works of Venn, Anderson and Allen, the concept of indigenization played a very minor role, in contrast to German missionary theory. The fact that the old formula; 'the Church must be rooted in the soil' has been replaced today by : 'the Church must be related to the soil', shows that modern missionary thinkers have remembered the Christological character of the Church.

On the other hand, we must admit that the further influence of the missionaries upon the young churches caused difficulties because, when organizing the Church, they followed, without thinking, the principles of their home Church. Henry Johnson saw clearly that to make the Ibo Church merely a copy of the Church of England would be to threaten its spiritual growth. The highly centralized church-constitution in Sumatra impeded the inner strengthening of the local congregations. Perhaps even more serious wounds were inflicted upon the Korean Church by the American Presbyterians who introduced into it their own legalistic, fundamentalist manner of interpreting the Bible, and carried into the mission-field American denominational differences which meant little or nothing to the Koreans.

Instead of waiting for the response which Nigeria, Sumatra and Korea would themselves make as being 'most agreeable to the Word of God', the missionaries dictated the answer which they themselves deemed appropriate, according to the tradition of the Anglican, Lutheran or Presbyterian Churches. On the other hand, Crowther's tactful attitude towards the customs of the Niger Delta, Nommensen's considerate treatment of Batak traditions, and the Presbyterian's tendency to preserve the Korean way of life, have no doubt facilitated the Church's ability to reach the people.

If we seek to examine these facts from a theological standpoint we must guard against coming to certain hasty conclusions. There is, for example, the difficult matter of relating God's activity in creation with His activity in redemption, above all in His redeeming activity in the development of the young Church. Admittedly both kinds of divine activity are present : it is the human beings whom God has created who are to be redeemed by Him. But we are not justified in imagining that divine revelation declares that particular social, political or racial phenomena are the products of God's continuing creative activity. History teaches us that nations and civilizations rise and fall, and that not even a Church which has identified itself completely with a particular civilization is able to purify and preserve that civilization. The Church must recognize that all earthly forms are impermanent; they belong to the order which is passing away, and this applies also to the outward forms of the Church itself which are similarly subject to change and, indeed, to final complete annihilation.

But against this, one must not overlook the fact that God's saving work is performed in history; it is what the Germans call *Heilsgeschichte,* the gradual revelation and realization of God's eschatological purpose in history. The statement 'the Word became flesh', for instance, means that God visits man in his historical and natural existence. Christ came to the Jews as a Jew, with all the characteristics of the Middle-Eastern people, attractive and unattractive to people of other communities and societies. He not only spoke His people's vernacular, His parables were based on their mentality and experience, and He showed them how one could become a re-born man in their situation. In the same spirit, St. Paul declares that he became 'all things to all men', to the Jews, as a Jew; to the weak, one who was himself weak. The Church must acknowledge that it is God who has created man in his historical circumstances and then try to translate the divine message into his language and ideology. This 'translation', however, is bound to break the framework of the existing culture and ideology because God has more to say to people than they can understand in terms of their own civilization and history.

The Church can never be satisfied simply with interpreting the historical situation in human terms, but must point men to an immeasurably greater, utterly different order. From this point of view, there are no historic forms of expression adequate to the Gospel. But that very fact entitles the indigenous tradition to be considered seriously and sympathetically as the agent through which the Gospel expresses itself in life, and that before any other possible agent is considered, as Dr. Kraemer has said. As this indigenous tradition is to be the agent of a new life it will not remain as it was. Its essence will be changed, and thus it will participate in the Gospel's foreignness in this world. Wherever the 'scandal' of the Gospel is no longer felt in an indigenous ecclesiastical form the Church is secularized; even, we may say, paganized. It has 'conformed to the fashion of this world' (Romans 12.2). It is significant that the Church of Rome, which teaches that there is a direct line from nature to grace, is most seriously affected by this process.

The objections to the foreign appearance of the Church on the mission-field do not apply only to certain externals of worship, like architecture and vestments, music and furnishings, nor are they directed only at Western forms of doctrine and organization : they are directed against the Western churches, as such. It is claimed that any definite organization, like an official ministry, or any firmly outlined dogma, are foreign to the Eastern mind and ought to give way to what is called 'spiritual freedom'. From the historical point of view, we must answer that the three great missionary churches we have been considering found that a firm organization, paid workers and a carefully formulated creed, were indispensable.

Azariah, the Indian bishop of Dornakal, agreed with this view. He acquired a great reputation as one of the most active champions of a truly Indian Church, yet he made this statement, which reminds us of Crowther's conservative attitude :

'The faith handed on to the saints, the Bible, the common confession of the Universal Church, the Sacraments, the historical ministry, the service and ritual of our parent Church are to be the heritage which we can continue to use and preserve for the Indian people.'

The objection we are discussing is understandable from the Hindu or Buddhist point of view, but completely misunderstands the New Testament character of the Church, which, as historical reality, requires the framework of an organization. Those connected with the Western Missions who repeat this objection may possibly do so, even unconsciously, because they think it will add to their popularity, but this is to misunderstand the experience of missionary history as well as the New Testament conception of the Church.

The Church, therefore, is a stranger in two respects. There is, on the one hand, what Dr. Freytag called 'the bondage of "Western peculiarities"'; the young Church must make a constant effort to break free from these, or at any rate from the false idea that these are inseparable from the Gospel, and the Western Mission ought to have the grace and humility to allow the Church to do so. On the other hand, the Church as a religious community is a stranger, by its very nature, in this world. Discarding this characteristic would mean it would no longer be the Church of Christ.

Both Continental and Anglo-American missionaries have repeatedly demanded that cultural and social elements found in the mission-field should be incorporated in the mission-Church, so as to help the young Church to become truly indigenous. We saw in the history of the Batak Church that this may coincide with widespread popular demand. It was the Batak who urged collective baptism, the preservation of ancient custom, and the giving of office in the government of the Church to local chiefs. We saw how, later, in the nationalist movement and the heathen renaissance, this trend was carried within the Church by the secular wave of anti-colonialism and in the political sphere by the assertion of national individuality.

J. C. Hoekendijk was not the first to protest against the identification of Church and Nation. During the nineteenth century pietist missionary thinkers who insisted on individual conversion objected to this identification. But since then the pietist theological position has been discredited by the facts of the psychology of religion. As Dr. Kraemer has pointed out, the results of our missionary experience and the findings of anthropology relevant to our investigation, do not permit us any longer to deny the fundamental fact that missionary work means an encounter with collective man. We saw unmistakably in the Batak missionary history that, although rarely nowadays, there can be a corporate call to conversion which fails to become a matter of personal challenge to the individual member of the group. Nevertheless in spite of all the disintegrating influences of modern life, local social groupings show a high degree of persistence, and there is no reason why the missionary should not use them as, what Donald McGavran calls, 'bridges of God'.

Yet it was the development in the Batak history which, in many points, confirmed the objections of the Pietist missionary thinkers. Wherever the horizontal line of natural ties was not crossed immediately after conversion by the vertical breakthrough of God's Word; where, that is, the individual was not affected, and the natural social ties not integrated into the new life, an adverse development was bound to follow. Firstly, the horizontal line neutralized the vertical; the national laws of life engulfed the call of the New Testament revelation. Secondly, the preservation of the national heritage was raised to the level of a theological standpoint so that syncretism resulted from the nationalist movement. The converts themselves felt the danger of syncretism most keenly. That is why, as Dr. Kraemer noticed, Western missionaries are more creative than nationals in making experiments with indigenous forms. Thirdly, where the 'acids of modernity' tended to disintegrate local social structures, the Church itself was endangered in so far as its own life was tied to these structures.

It would be interesting to conjecture what would have happened to the Korean Church—the historical ties of half of whose members have been broken since 1945—if these ties had been an integral part of her structure. The fact that a new Church arose in all the refugee and prisoner-of-war camps is a proof that the Church had not been held together by the ties of race and soil, but by faith, hope and love in the Gospel.

Passages like Matthew 16.18; I Corinthians 3.11 and Ephesians 2.20 disprove the conception of the 'old foundations'; nor can one apply the simile of the 'lively stones' (I Peter 2.5) to the national culture and institutions. The missionaries' policy of integrating national heritage in the Church in Sumatra was based on the idea of a direct relation between the realm of nature and that of grace, taught by some of the medieval scholastic thinkers, but not warranted by the Gospel.

If we reject the policy of incorporating national traditions into the young Church, that does not mean we are prepared to oppose the very idea of an indigenous character for the Church; the rejection is rather intended as a corrective. Before we decide how to make the Church truly indigenous we must define what we mean by an 'indigenous Church'. The missionary scholars who have championed the idea of a truly indigenous Church so far, actuated by a certain romanticism, have been more interested in preserving what already existed than in trying to define the nature of the Church which is indigenous. Allen's common-sense in regarding the indigenous character of the young Church as nothing but its external freedom from foreign control and its ability to live and propagate the Gospel sucessfully in its own country, deserves special note. The missionary history of Sumatra and Korea bears out Kraemer's statement :

> 'The way towards becoming an indigenous Church goes first through becoming a real *Church*.'

The process of indigenization in the Niger Delta began with local Christians building mud-chapels in the hinterland of the mission-stations and preaching to their pagan countrymen there, without any official authority. The missionary Gospel penetrated the Batak nation when Batak evangelists began to translate it into their own vivid language with its wealth of imagery. The same thing happened in Korea, when Christian peasants, witnessing voluntarily, entered their neighbours' houses to tell of their faith, thus forming the typical Korean house-congregations.

Local church-architecture was not created by the missionaries' artistic efforts, but by the young Christians who built chapels, for which they had given the money, and which they naturally erected in a style familiar to the local people. In the course of a church's history further indigenous forms evolve. The typical polyphonous prayer of the Koreans and their prayer-meetings at night are a result of the great revival of 1907-8. The Batak colonists' mission, and the Koreans' Bible-classes in the camps, are genuine forms of up-to-date native Christianity which simply consists in an active response to the tasks of the actual situation.

From all this, we may deduce that no part of the cultural heritage can be regarded as an uncorrupted expression of God's creation; anything that is to be incorporated into the Church as an expression of the Word must first be transformed by the Gospel. However, there are various degrees of religious significance in the national heritage. On the other hand, the young Christians are not all equally liable to be tempted by manifestations of the old religion, and the missionaries do not always know the danger zone. Hence we are led to agree with Kraemer that 'only the converted spirit of the nationals' can convert the traditional way of life and give it a new content. It appears that the ratio between heathen infection of tradition and the Christians' power of resistance changes in favour of the latter if the Church grows normally, and this helps to promote a truly indigenous form.

It is essential, therefore, that the foreign missionary should avoid giving the impression that only his own native forms of worship and architecture, his own method of dealing with theological problems, his own traditions of administration, are truly Christian. Further, it is essential that he be cautious not to disturb the results of a genuinely spiritual movement of indigenous Christianity. Wherever men have found faith, and have realized that they themselves are messengers and are sent to their non-Christian neighbours, their message will quite naturally assume forms understood in their own country or social environment.

The task of making the Church truly indigenous is naturally a delicate one, requiring the skill to avoid the Scylla of a simple absorption into the national tradition and the Charybdis of being paralysed by compulsory Westernization. The Church becomes indigenous by responding obediently to God's call in the contemporary and local circumstances and by complete and truly Christian identification with those to whom the Church is commanded to proclaim the Gospel. As Christ is the Lord of creation, there is, in theory, no part of creation which He cannot make an agent of His Word. But, as the original creation stands now under the judgement of God, there can never be a completely indigenous Church in the world, for the Church, like the Gospel, must always be something of a stumbling-block, a *skandalon,* in the world.

For many years the debate concerning the responsible selfhood of the Church has dealt primarily with the autonomy of the younger churches over against the paternalistic direction of Western missions. More recently, however, it has been made plain that the danger to the Church comes not so much from Western missions—nearly all of which are committed to principles like 'partnership in obedience' and 'integration'—as from political, economic and social factors in the local environment itself. In this situation, the Church, like that of the first century, is tempted to look upon the State as Antichrist and to retire into a sort of 'ghetto'. But the Church is called not only out of the world but also into the world, to maintain not only its independence of all earthly traditions and authority but to redeem those traditions and powers and to give its own life 'a ransom for many'.

The early Anglican, German and American Missions we have studied agreed in regarding as the objects of their work, not the individual Ibo, Batak or Korean, close to their mission-stations, but the whole population of the country. They realized that historical and social relations were of importance to the Church; hence they planned missionary strategy with the whole of the Niger, Batak or Korean territories in view. But the difference was that Crowther and the Rhenish missionaries thought of the nation, while the American Presbyterians thought of the geographical area. That is why Crowther and the Rhenish missionaries appealed first to the local chiefs as the representatives of society, whereas the Presbyterians appealed to the Koreans as individuals. The result was that, however distant the goal envisaged by the Presbyterians, it remained an individualist one : they talked of 'a million souls for Christ', and paid no attention to the social relations which bound these individual souls into a society. This difference affected the missionary spirit of the young churches.

The *Kongsi Batak,* founded in 1900, was intended to be supported exclusively by Batak and to work among the Batak. The chief impetus of the *Zending Batak* was its national and missionary responsibility for the Batak dispersion. But this national emphasis was at the same time a limitation.

The Nigerians never managed to extend their mission beyond their own borders and their own people. That this is a special danger inherent in a national Church is proved by the example of the German Gossner Evangelical Lutheran Church in India. W. Niesel of the German Evangelical Church reported concerning his visit to that Church, that he heard young pastors earnestly reminded that they were to carry the Gospel to everyone without distinction, whether caste Hindus or outcastes. The fact that such distinctions, originating in ancient non-Christian social tensions, tend still to persist in parts of the Indian Church impedes the spread of the Gospel.

'The leaders of the young Church which has just freed itself from the white man's tutelage must now in quite a different situation pronounce a Christian warning to those whose national consciousness has been re-awakened.'

The case in Korea was different. The fact that the Mission was directed towards individual souls prevented an excessive emphasis on the nation, as such. Therefore, from 1912 Korea had its own foreign mission, which seemed a senseless waste of energy, but was of importance because it showed that the Koreans understood the nature of Mission. They remained aware of the real boundary between the Church and the World. The experiences of recent Batak missionary history prove that this awareness can be obscured if the missionary concept is a purely national one. The leader of the *Batak Saksi ni Kristus* claims that one group of Batak Christians, the Simalungum, possess a stronger missionary impetus than another group, the Tobanese, because the latter joined, and still join, the Church in groups, whereas the former join it singly. If a group is converted, that group is preserved within the Church, unless it is intentionally disintegrated and this tends to give the members an introverted attitude. Only if the Christian is aware of this fundamental contrast will his necessary missionary concern for his own nation remain pure.

Although the Gospel of the Kingdom of Heaven is eschatological, it also has a strong social dynamic with which to charge the world. We saw, on the Niger, in Sumatra and in Korea, that missionary preaching almost automatically has social and political implications which far surpass the limits of 'church-life' in the narrow sense of the term. Economic prosperity, the halting of long-standing feuds, and the emancipation of women were some of these. Although it was not an item in the missionary programme, Christian stewardship led to a new attitude to the daily occupation and the family life of the Christian.

But the missionaries, at least in Sumatra and Korea, aimed at more : they wanted to make the young Church aware of the social aspect of the Gospel and to train it to undertake charitable and cultural tasks. Strangely enough, their initial efforts failed both in Sumatra and in Korea. The situation was different in Crowther's Niger Mission, where the agents, and with them the young Christians, had to struggle from the start to save the lives of foundlings, old women and human victims designated for sacrifice. In contrast to this, the Batak Church temporarily gave up its charitable institutions, whilst the Korean Church refused to begin any such work. There are two reasons for this : the first is the almost ineradicable selfishness of the old Adam, causing man to neglect his needy brother, and the second, and, in our opinion, more important, is the vagueness in the missionaries' explanation of the social aspect of the Gospel. Faith and love were separated, in spite of all the diligent Bible-study.

Thus, in many places, the medical mission became a separate missionary enterprise, apart from the Church. Not until they experienced the war and the post-war period did the young churches in the two countries open their eyes to their social responsibilities. Out of this experience the churches realized that they could not by-pass social problems. If only to maintain themselves as an integral and relevant part of the nation's life, the churches were compelled to come out of their ghettoes and to proclaim the Gospel to the nation, in Christian service and in the full discharge of the duties of Christian citizenship.

How far does the social duty of the young Church extend? On the Niger, in Sumatra and in Korea, the abortive attempt was made to identify the Christian community with the civil community. There is in the Gospel no detailed scheme for solving social problems. Crowther was unable himself to fulfil the promises he had made in this respect, and similar projects of the American pioneer missionaries only brought disappointment to the Koreans. Nommensen, who introduced ecclesiastical and civil order simultaneously, thus achieved a partial fusion of the Christian and civil communities, and this is still a cause of trouble in the Batak Church, for in this way church-discipline came to be exercised in a legalistic manner. The *aturan* (custom) was given undue authority, and the young Church was not completely successful in asserting her spiritual nature when challenged by nationalism.

It is not the duty of the Church, but of the State, to create a social and political order. That must be clearly asserted in contradiction to Davis's socio-economic missionary theory. The Church, based on revelation, has no revealed political or social programme, nor, as a Church, has it the means to put such a programme into effect, even if it had one. But the Church, aware of the imperfection of all human order, is responsible for maintaining and constantly correcting it. In this task, the Church's only instruments are Christian witness and brotherly love, and these overcome all selfishness, self-importance and legalism. Like the healing acts of Christ, the social activity of the Church is not an end in itself but is also a means to a higher end, as a mark of a higher order of life, of which here below only the bare rudiments can be realized.

Only the awareness of this eschatological limitation, this understanding of the Church's ministry of compassion as witness to the fact that the Kingdom of God has 'broken through' into the natural order, can save the Church from a purely secular attitude to its service to humanity. The Church performs acts of humanitarian service out of loving concern for 'the least of these my brethren', not just to make this world a better place, but because it is aware that every needy person is by right, and in actual fact, a member of the new eschatological family, the family which God has already created in Christ, the 'first-born of many brethren'. Thus the fellowship of the redeemed community gives the non-Christian the most convincing proof that life in this world can be redeemed, transfigured. St. Paul conceives this fellowship (*koinonia*) just as realistically as Davis does (cf I Thessalonians 4.10; II Thessalonians 3.3-16). From the founding of the very first Christian congregation, and through all the ages, this 'fellowship of the mystery' has been a main reason for the spontaneous expansion of the Church.

Because of its apostolic and prophetic duties, the Church must avoid becoming dependent on the nation. But its selfhood may easily be threatened by the State. In three ways the Church may lose its liberty to the powers of this world : by external dependence, by persecution, and by political temptation.

The mission Church falls into external dependence upon the State if there is a question of government recognition and protection. Very few mission-churches will be able to avoid this completely, for, if the Church renounces government recognition in order to work in complete independence, this may well lead to the Church's being declared an illegal organization and a mission-Church will take this step only in the most exceptional circumstances. The sole problem is, therefore, how far the mission-Church may accept political protection without a conflict of loyalty. The decisive question will always be : is the mission-Church actuated by sordid opportunism, or does it really only intend to give unto Caesar the things that are Caesar's?

Another form of dependence upon the Government is the widespread practice among mission-churches of accepting State subsidies. The history of the Batak mission in the 1920s shows unmistakably what may be the result for the spread of the Gospel if the Church accepts these subsidies without question. An even clearer case is the acceptance of subsidies for schools which almost destroyed the pastoral system of the young Batak Church. That proves the truth of one observer's statement :

'As long as a Church is directly or indirectly dependent financially upon the Government, or exists on Government privileges, there can be no question of an autonomous Church.'

Comparing the Batak with the Korean Church, only one conclusion can be drawn : the mission Church must be ready and able to carry out all specifically ecclesiastical duties from the start, without recourse to outside financial help.

In times of persecution, the State, or other hostile political powers, may try forcibly to deprive the young Church of ecclesiastical selfhood, by prohibiting the conduct of public worship including the preaching of the Word, as well as in other ways. But not even the most ruthless persecution can deprive an obedient Church of its responsible selfhood, for this consists solely in the Church's union with its Head, a union no external power can destroy.

Political temptation is even more dangerous than political persecution. In the case of persecution, at least the Church can recognize an enemy for what he is, but the temptation to conform to the world, to become coloured by political aims and ideologies, is more subtle and infinitely more deadly. 'Fear not him who has power to kill the body, but rather him that has power to destroy both body and soul'. This happens when the Church sees itself as a human organization simply, into which all secular movements can be incorporated without first being completely transformed by the Gospel. Perhaps the most outstanding example of this temptation, particularly in the case of the churches of Asia and Africa, is that which arises from nationalism, even though Merle Davis still classes it among the most important 'resources for self-support'. The part played by nationalism in the Batak Church makes this danger clear.

We freely grant that nationalism has a critical function in relation to the Church. It can, for example, call the Mission to repentance for its overbearing domination of the young Church. But nationalism itself is not a determining factor in the nature and constitution of the Church. In the first place, it isolates the young national Church from the ecumenical fellowship of the world Church, and causes chain-reactions, making for further separatist movements. Secondly, nationalism causes spiritual anaemia in the young Church and leads to spiritual perversion, as in the case of some of the Bantu sects in Africa which Sundkler calls 'broken branches, desiccated churches'.

As the Chinese experience proves, Protestant mission-churches are more exposed to the danger of nationalist isolation than are Roman Catholic churches, for, from their inception, the Protestant churches had put before them the slogan of the 'three selves', which is fundamentally a proclamation of organizational independence. It would, however, be superficial to find the root of this evil in Venn's and Anderson's conception of autonomy, for Venn and Anderson were inspired by the model of their own churches which were all national, or at least independent, churches.

If we look for the root of the nationalist problem in our present mission-churches, we must go back to the Reformation era when the Reformers' conception of the Church, though fundamentally ecumenical, could not develop because of the strong nationalist ideology of that age, but instead degenerated into a national or State Church. This development was facilitated theologically by the fact that the Reformers, while restoring the New Testament faith, were yet not able to formulate unequivocally ecumenical church-order. Thus Luther, in his 'Doctrine of the Two Realms', based on Romans 13 and the teaching of St. Augustine of Hippo, made a clear division between spiritual and secular power. But, as we have already indicated, the church-situation forced Luther to obscure this by claiming emergency measures, which led to the regional prince supervising the Church. Theoretically, that contradicted and even cancelled out Luther's own theory of the 'Two Realms'.

Considered under this wider aspect, the problem of the autonomy of the younger churches, caused by non-European nationalism, cannot be treated purely from the point of view of the principles of missions. It is inextricably linked with the controversy over 'Faith and Order' in the ecumenical movement.

Chapter 9

THE UNITY OF THE CHURCH AND THE
AUTONOMY OF ITS MEMBERS

Since we have again learnt to regard mission as the decisive function of the whole Church, we must consider the problem of the young Church's constitutional autonomy within the wider framework of the whole Church, and not just as a peculiar problem affecting foreign missions. The young Church has to grapple with this problem from three different aspects. There is first the local aspect, namely the relation between the local congregation, the regional Church body and the Universal Church. Secondly there is what may be called the historical or genealogical aspect, that is, the relation between the young Church and its parent Church or Mission. The third aspect is the denominational one, affecting the young Church's attempts to find the right relation with other denominations, especially in its own country. Only if all those aspects are taken into account, can we realize the full scope of the problem. Let us first consider, then, the nature of the young Church's constitutional organization within the framework of the Church Universal.

We defined the selfhood of the young Church as its power, readiness and freedom to follow its divine call within its sphere of life. Thus, selfhood depends on the call. What has been stated already concerning this call applies to the Church, as such. But, according to both the Old Testament and the New Testament, the true Church is both the Church Universal, (the total number of those called by God) and also the local manifestation of the Church Universal, however small or weak. Does this mean that the local Church can turn only as a small cog in the huge wheel of the Church Universal? Or, conversely, that the local Church, because it is a genuine Church by reason of the presence within it of the Word and the Sacraments, need take no notice of the existence of the Church Universal? Is there a visible organic relation between the local Church and the Church Universal, and, if so, what is that relation? That is the problem underlying the dispute about the right church-order. What does it mean that every local Church belongs directly to Christ, yet is only part of His Body?

Although its missionary origin shows that the Church Universal exists prior to the local Church, nevertheless it has its first genuine experience of the nature of the Church within the local Church. It is in the worship, fellowship, and witness of the local congregation, and not in the administrative super-structure created by the missionaries, that the true nature of the Church is seen. Here, the priesthood of all believers is made effectively visible. It took only a short time for a true Church in this sense, however small, to grow out of missionary preaching, but it was more difficult to form an administrative organization for groups of such congregations with local resources and local leaders.

This experience seemed to support the missionaries' argument against the early granting of autonomy to young churches, namely that the local Christians were unable to maintain and operate the centralized organization of the Church which they, the missionaries, themselves had created. The conclusion is correct, but the pre-suppositions are wrong. We have already seen that the imposition of the burden of such an organization upon the young Christians is premature and unreasonable, leading to unpleasant tensions in the life of the Church.

A comparison between the Presbyterian Mission in Korea, and the work in Nigeria or among the Batak, shows us that those tensions are not unavoidable. The Presbyterians not only called the local congregations 'churches', they entrusted them with the bulk of the Church's activities. Hence, they never experienced the difficulties of the Niger and Batak churches in finding local Christians capable of holding positions of responsibility in the Church. The Anglican and the German missionaries, on the other hand, regarded the central organization, rather than the local congregation, as 'the Church'. Shortly before his death, Johannes Warneck made a revealing statement :

'The beginning is the miracle of the converted individual; then comes the miracle of the local congregation, then the miracle of the Church and finally, as the climax, the miracle of the communion of saints throughout all nations and races.'

There is nothing in the New Testament to justify any such distinction between congregation and Church. For the New Testament, the administrative organization has no theological relevance for the understanding of the meaning of *ecclesia*. Wherever this term is used with an administrative connotation it applies directly to the local congregation, never to a council or 'committee'. St. Paul never uses expressions like 'The Church in Asia' or 'the Church in Macedonia'; he always uses the plural, churches, when referring to the Christian cause in a geographical area wider than the local unit.

The theological imagery applied to the Church : people, body, temple, priesthood, etc. almost invariably refers to the local congregation, or else to all such congregations in the world. It does not apply to an administrative organization, and this, not because such an organization does not, in fact, exist, but because it was not, even if it did exist, to be identified with the Church. The fact that it is virtually, if not completely, identified with the Church in so many parts of Asia and Africa today is one of the most striking and truly grievous examples of the divergence between New Testament teaching and missionary policy.

We see a germ of this attitude already in the writings of Ignatius in the second century; although he still regarded the local Church as the *ecclesia,* he was the first to lay stress on the episcopal office, and thus to make the administrative and constitutional aspect of the Church an integral part of the Church's being. The logical development of this conception is thus to be seen in the progress from congregation to diocese, patriarchate, and, finally, to the papacy. Luther's criticism of the idea of the Church as an administrative, let alone legislative body, with powers of jurisdiction in its own proper field, was not universally accepted.

Venn and Gustav Warneck introduce the administrative conception of the Church into missionary theory, and so they led to those unhappy tensions and resistances which we have noted. If we want to take an unprejudiced view of the problem of the responsible selfhood of the Church we must again learn from

St. Paul that the *ecclesia* is, first of all, the local Church, and that all superior administrative offices and organizations exist for the sole purpose of building up the life of the local Church in fellowship with other similar congregations.

Every truly reformed church-order will begin with the local Church as the basis of its organization. It is on the local level that the corporate, as well as the individual, functions of the 'priesthood of all believers' are to be demonstrated to the world : in public and in private worship, in brotherly service, pastoral care, church-discipline, and in witness in word and deed. The special offices of pastor, elder and other church-workers, who concentrate on particular aspects of the Church's life, must be emphasized. These offices, conferred by ordination or other solemn form of commissioning, are very numerous in the younger churches, but they must never take the place of the spiritual ministry of the whole community. Although in most places supra-local rules and written constitutions come quite soon to be drafted for the Church's nurture and discipline, we must always respect the liberty of the local congregation which has its origin in the spiritual influence of the Gospel.

As to financial autonomy, we can start with the principle of Nommensen and Nevius, also propagated by Allen, that fundamentally each local congregation has to be fully self-supporting from the beginning, as far as its own work is concerned, with the funds administered by the elders or other officers. The financial resources of the local Church determine how long it has to rely on unpaid voluntary service from its officers.

At the same time, the local Church must be conscious of its responsibilities beyond its own immediate sphere, and that for two reasons.

First, the local Church must actively acknowledge its share of the responsibility for proclaiming the Gospel, not only within its own confines but throughout the whole world; it must not only join in prayer for others, but must, from the start, offer material gifts for this wider work. Contrasting the experiences of the Batak and the Korean Churches, the system whereby the church-members themselves assess the amount of their own church-contribution, stimulated by confrontation with their tasks, seems one to be recommended.

Secondly, there is nothing to prevent the local Church from receiving assistance from the whole Church in certain emergencies, such as those caused by sudden disasters or by sudden developments in the Church's work. The demand for self-support must never turn into a demand for financial autonomy, under all circumstances, either in the case of the local Church or in that of the national Church.

The task and relations of the local Church beyond its own borders further imply, in concrete terms, that the Church again and again has to send some of its members for missionary service beyond its own area. They also involve the Church in the responsibility for sending representatives to undertake some of the work of the regional Church and also for listening to the pronouncements of the regional Church.

In Sumatra, Korea and on the Niger, the local churches, at quite an early stage, thought not only of themselves but of each other. This was caused partly by their belonging to the same political or social unit, partly by the missionaries and native evangelists who served as links between the different congregations and areas. Soon, the local congregations realized that questions and tasks concerning them all had best be discussed and solved together. These synods were attended by delegates who together listened to the Word, together tried to solve their common problems.

The essence of the Church's life in obedience to Christ is listening to and obeying His call; it is the local Church which first experiences His Lordship, but this forms a link with, not a separation from, the other local churches and with the world Church. The Church of Christ is not concerned with the opposition between rival forms of church-government, but it is vitally concerned to recognize that forms, which are often championed by fanatical supporters in opposition to others, are, with those others, essential to the building up of the Body of Christ.

The history of Missions, not least the history of the three churches which we have been specially considering, provides fairly conclusive demonstration that Congregational, Presbyterian and Episcopal forms of church-government have all an essential place in the life of the Church : any single form becomes distorted, and therefore ineffective, when emphasized to the exclusion of the others. Modern schemes of Church Union all proceed on this basic assumption, but it is an assumption that has come into the heritage and experience of the Church 'not without dust and heat'. There is no value whatsoever in any discussion of the 'responsible selfhood of the Church' which ignores this unshakable conviction based on the history of the modern missionary and ecumenical movements.

St. Paul's writings lend much support to the view we have expressed; that the Church is not to be confused with its administrative machinery or regional organization. St. Paul did not create regional church-organizations, but he has three positive things to say :

1. He sees the unity of his local churches, above all, in the one Apostolic Message. 'What? Came the Word of God out from you? Or came it unto you only?' (I Corinthians 14.36). The Word brings into being the common understanding, the common order and the common apostolic and prophetic responsibility of the churches. As the local churches are aware of the supra-local authority of the Word, they are ready to submit to correction; their freedom is not freedom from God's law but freedom to act in God's Name.

2. The unity of the local churches is not the 'pre-established harmony of hermetically sealed monads', of the kind taught by the German philosopher Leibniz. Rather, is it *koinonia,* the common life of the body of Christ, mutual brotherly help in word and deed. St. Paul encouraged the local churches to meet on occasion and thus strengthened their feeling of unity. By collecting money for the parent Church he combatted Christian collective selfishness, which already existed in his time. Self-support was not enough for him.

3. The common life of the local churches consisted in their common missionary work, in the extension of which the Christians of all regions showed active concern (I Thessalonians 1.8). St. Paul did not see the three dimensions of the Church limited to the region any more than to the local congregation. Admittedly, he regards the local congregations of any one particular region as, in certain respects, working units; but he did everything possible to create a close contact between the different regions in order to help them experience something of the ecumenical life of the Church Universal.

What are we to deduce from all this, concerning church-order? First of all, we can make the negative deduction that it is not the organizational unit, the constitutional framework of a regional Church which makes the local congregations in a certain area truly churches.

'But if a responsible mission joins the separate congregations of a mission area into a "Church" the mission must realize that in founding this "Church" it really only renders visible something that already existed long before.'

We shall have to agree with this statement of Johannes Dürr's, even if the young Christians in a mission-area themselves conceive the constitution as an integral and indispensable part of the Church. In-so-far as this is not clearly and directly the result of missionary influence, the young Christians have formed their conception of the Church in analogy with political constitutions and have thus drawn the wrong conclusion. The life-blood of a Church under the rule of Christ circulates wherever Christians live.

But although a 'supra-local' constitution does not make a Church, it is essential to create such a constitution in order to put into effect supra-local unity of the Church in its common life and work. This constitution is only of value if the local churches can deduce from it that the tasks of the supra-local Church are their own tasks, for which all Christians are jointly responsible. If, therefore, this regional organization has an assembly capable of passing resolutions, this must be a synod in which delegates from the local churches discuss matters of common importance. Their common ground is both the Word, which has come to all local churches, and the common external situation to which the universal Word is to be applied. Such external common interests, which necessitate the formation of special units of church-workers, exist at various levels.

A world-wide, truly ecumenical synod is the ultimate aim, and a national or tribal Church must not erect any barriers which would hinder this ultimate achievement. With this proviso, there is a great deal to be said for making the national or regional synod a very powerful working unit. Language, civilization, history, social and educational traditions, problems of home and foreign policy, constitute a community so closely knit together that the Church must direct its message and method towards these factors. If the national Church is thus conceived, as a missionary programme, as was implicitly done by all the German missionary thinkers, it must be accepted.

It ought to be understood that the nation is not to be regarded as the structural basis of the Church, nor that the Church should form an integral part of the nation. Rather, the nation is the historic environment which demands the highest degree of attuning (not, be it noted, 'adaptation' or 'becoming rooted') on the part of the Church. In the growth of mission-churches it will be inevitable that the local churches of a nation form a national synod which lays down rules valid for all.

This synod appoints some of its members to a number of committees, on behalf of the whole Church. The most important of them is the executive committee of the synod. In addition, there is a number of other bodies occupied with the various practical tasks and responsibilities of the Church as a whole : home and foreign missions, youth work, training of ministers and other church-workers, social, educational and literature-work, as well as ecumenical enterprises and organizations.

These bodies have no right to exist unless they are firmly rooted in the local churches in whose name they act. This must be stressed because they are so often in danger of trying to act independently, claiming that the technical complications of their respective spheres of responsibility make this necessary. Thus they tend to act as societies apart from, or even superior to, the local churches with which their main contact is a purely financial one. Hence, foreign missions and other forms of service must not be left to a special circle of friends within the local Church, but must be the concern of the entire Church.

The supra-local organization of the Church has not only the authority to pass resolutions : it serves at the same time to edify the members spiritually and to strengthen them as a fellowship of brethren. Technical difficulties render it impossible to do this on a national basis : hence frequent regional meetings need to be held.

While dealing with the church-order of the mission-churches, we have to ask again when the young churches are ready for independence. As we have already said in an earlier chapter, as the Church grows spiritually and administratively its tasks increase.

Thus the district synods will be the first to be created, but soon afterwards the general synod of the whole region requires setting up.

In view of the Church's ecumenical nature, there is no reason why missionaries should not be members of the general synod. The Korean system appears the most organic, in which native Christians gradually out-number the missionaries on ecclesiastical boards so that the latter withdraw to a mainly advisory capacity. The synod ought to decide whether administrative posts are to be filled by missionaries or native Christians.

If the synod insists on missionaries occupying leading positions, the latter ought to train native Christians to take over in an emergency. On the other hand, nationals in leading positions are likely to be aware of their own lack of experience where this is, in fact, the case, and, in such circumstances, they will wisely avail themselves of the good counsel of experienced missionaries. The whole question hangs, not on nationality but on experience, so that, in the same way, an inexperienced missionary, if wise, will turn to an experienced national for advice.

In seeking to define the constitutional autonomy of the young Church, in its local and wider aspects, we have taken so far the already existing local churches as a basis for discussion. But no Church comes into being without any mediation of, or connexion with, the already existing Universal Church. Only the fact that the young Church conforms to the Universal Church in regard to the Word, and shares in spreading it, proves that the young Church is really a genuine Church. The fact that it is Christ Himself who builds the Church in the mission-field, as elsewhere, prevents the young Church from being entirely independent of the Universal Church.

The Church of Christ is one, and the young Church can claim to be His Church only in so far as it is an organic part of the Church Universal. That this was the view of the Apostles is demonstrated by the sending of Barnabas from Jerusalem to the new local Church at Antioch (Acts 11.22-26). This incident seems to have been of decisive importance for the early Christians' conception of the relation between the Church Universal and the 'mission Church'.

Turning to the question of the Church's faith, we recall the importance given to autonomy in matters of belief in Warneck's and Allen's teaching, and in the confessional struggles of the young churches in Sumatra and Korea. Allen, convinced that the Gospel is essentially not doctrine but power and life, (in contrast with Warneck, for whom right doctrine was of central importance) waived the claim of the founding mission to insist on its own particular doctrines being adhered to by the young Church. He felt that divine grace, or rather the indwelling Spirit, would, reinforced by Christian experience, lead the members of the young Church to the right doctrinal teaching without any outside help. This is not borne out by early Christian history. If Allen were right, it would have been unnecessary for Barnabas to go to Antioch, much less to stay there. The grace of God and the consequent inner experiences of faith on the part of local churches would have released him from the necessity to teach there. In fact, he remained at Antioch because he had to teach (Acts 11.26).

Following the New Testament, we must make a clear distinction between proclaiming the message of salvation, which calls men and awakens their faith, thus founding the Church, and teaching the Word which strengthens the faith of the Church. We can deduce from this that there can be no autonomy of doctrine in the Church, not even when, by faith, the direct connexion of every believer with Christ has been established. The handing down of doctrine, not only to the local Church as a whole, (I Corinthians 11.23; 15.1-3) but especially to the officers and teachers of the congregations, plays a major part in the New Testament. This, however, cannot be understood as handing over the Bible, for, whereas the larger local churches certainly had the Old Testament, St. Paul regarded his epistles merely as occasional writings. Even in those days it would not have been impossible to make a written collection of apostolic doctrinal utterances and to distribute copies of these. What in fact happened was the handing on of doctrine by direct oral instruction, first to teachers and officers of the congregations, and then to all the members. That led to the first wording of the doctrinal confession in the early Church and to the drafting of the rule of faith in the postapostolic era.

There can be no doctrinal autonomy in the Church, in-so-far

as the Church relies upon the authority of the Bible. It would be wrong of the young Church to rely on its conscience simply, or on its own experience of the indwelling Spirit, for, in the first case, a human authority would be set up as the standard of doctrine, and, in the second case, the young Church's experience of the indwelling Spirit is set up against the similar experience of the parent Church which formulated the denominational statement of faith.

The church-order of a young Church must have something positive to say about the confession of the Church. First, it has to adopt the ecumenical confessions of the early Church, whose validity is still almost universally accepted. The situation is more difficult with regard to the denominational confessions, drawn up in later generations. They too, however, claim, not only to reflect the doctrine of the denomination in question, but to be valid interpretations of Scripture, the basis for the doctrinal unity of the Church in all ages. Admittedly, many of these confessions suffer by contradicting one another, so that their claim cannot be regarded as absolute : yet the young Church will probably have to accept these confessions, at least provisionally, so far as their contents do not obviously contradict its own understanding of Scripture. This is necessary in order to have some historical visible link with a present branch of the Church, and, through it, with the early Church.

The fact that there are other denominational confessions will be a cause of constant disquiet to the young Church, and will remind it of the painful disunity within the Universal Church, for which the young Church will now have to acknowledge a share of responsibility. It must be a sacred task for the young Church to help to heal this disunity.

One of the most important questions left open in Part II of this study, because of the discrepancies of the missionary theories examined in Part I, was whether the exercise of authority, on the part of the young Church, was to be limited to local church-officers, or the local organization as a whole, or whether the Church should have supra-local officers. The Korea Mission of the American Presbyterian Church, a denomination with a pronounced tendency to decentralization, regarded an efficient system of supervision as one of the essential conditions for the

11

success of Nevius' method, as practised there. The Niger Mission broke down because Bishop Crowther was unable to inspect his young stations frequently and regularly.

It seems to be the universal experience of all Protestant missions that the congregational principle cannot be put into practice by itself in the mission-field. Even the Independents, as we saw in Anderson's case, have found themselves forced to resort, at least temporarily, to a centralized system in order to guarantee the stability of what they had created. Moreover, episcopacy has a strong appeal in nearly all mission-fields, even where the actual term is not used, as for example in Sumatra. To the student of missions that throws a new light on the New Testament pronouncements concerning the problem of church-order.

New Testament scholars have known for a long time that there were, in the early Church, at least three supra-congregational ministries, namely those of apostles, teachers and prophets. According to Ephesians 4.12 these three functions in the Church aim at the perfecting of the saints for the work of the ministry. The apostles and teachers were in uninterrupted contact with each other about their responsibilities in the Church as a whole. Those who exercised these functions—i.e. first of all the apostles, but after them the teachers—had indeed the highest authority in the primitive Church, as we can see from the examples of Barnabas and Apollos.

The functions of the first apostles were threefold.

Firstly, they had to formulate the message of salvation on which the Church was founded in a way that would be permanently valid. In this function they could not be succeeded, and, through it, they, together with the Old Testament prophets, formed the basis on which the Church was built (Ephesians 2.20). Secondly, they were called to proclaim the message in the world and to found the world-wide Church upon it. Thirdly, through their ministry they were entrusted with the constant responsibility for the whole Church.

Accordingly, and this is particularly clear in St. Paul's epistles, the apostles claimed an authority that was limited by nothing save the Word whose messengers they were.

In spite of that, the authority of the apostles implied no magisterial power. Their missionary service included the organization of everything connected with doctrine, worship and church-order, but their aim was that the local churches, once having been taught the principles, should adopt and practise them on their own. St. Paul did not consider it one of his permanent duties to intervene in cases of church-discipline. It is apparent that the two last-named functions of the apostles—proclamation and visitation—are vital in the Church, not only in the early era.

Ever since Calvin, who declared that the ministry of the apostles ceased with them, Protestant theologians have tried to discount the idea that the apostles had any successors in their ministry. Sound biblical interpretation, however, does not bear this out. Calvin was right in denying that the historical Episcopate is simply the continuation of the apostles' ministry, because in the Episcopate the ecumenical functions of the apostles and the administrative functions of the presbyters have been merged. He was wrong, however, in his belief that the apostles had no successors at all.

This combination of administrative functions, representing the responsibility of all the members of a local Church with the ministry of teaching and visiting, which originally belonged to the Church as a whole, led to a centralizing of authority in the episcopal office, about which Protestants were later to have such deep misgivings.

Many Protestants did away with episcopacy in their church-organizations. Where episcopacy has been preserved in Protestant denominations its apostolic character is no longer clearly seen. The bishop in these churches is either simply the administrative head of a synodal system, or he is surrounded with a mystical aura which is supposed to reflect, and to guarantee, the mysterious connexion of the Church today with that which has existed throughout the ages. The mystical union of the Church is through the bishop, rather than through the continuing tradition of orthodox teaching.

It is not surprising, therefore, that in such church-circles there tends to be some lack of concern for orthodox teaching, a lack which is in sharp contrast with the rabbinical origin of the Christian system of succession. Among the rabbis, ordination had always to be preceded by the teacher handing on the doctrine to his disciple, and, in the Church, there can be a true succession of ministry through the ages only if those who are commissioned to guide and extend the Church have embraced, not only the true spirit of the apostles, but also their basic doctrine.

The apostolic ministry can be a living reality today only if the various chains of succession, including that of the faithful in their acknowledgment of Christian belief, are joined together. In this connexion we may observe that the provision of a service of mutual commissioning, as in the Plan for Church Union in North India and in the proposals in uniting Anglicans and Methodists in England is not to be regarded as a bait in an Anglican trap, but as an honest and effective means of joining together several incomplete and separate chains in the succession of the one Church.

The young Church needs a supra-local ministry of oversight which forms a historical and organizational link with the Church Universal. It must be stressed that the essential features of this office are teaching, and, through it, the oversight of the whole Church, pastoral care of the brethren, and authority to ordain. This office need not assume a monarchical form. In the New Testament times the function of oversight (*episcopé*) could be related to a single congregation or to a number of congregations, and these different forms of the one function complemented each other and could be substituted for one another.

If episcopacy is thus interpreted, the vexed question of when it can properly be introduced into the young mission-Church finds a comprehensive answer. In spite of the pointless dispute about the name, the young Church, even where the diocesan bishop is, to begin with, a foreign missionary, will have its own 'bishops'. By accompanying the missionary-bishops or district-missionaries, these will learn to assist them in their work, just as St. Paul's fellow-workers went about with him and co-operated with him. As the young Church grows in obedience to Christ's rule, so will its shepherds and their shepherds, the *pastores pastorum,* and so will their authority increase.

Chapter 10

DAUGHTER CHURCH AND PARENT CHURCH

IN CONTRAST with Venn's abortive attempt to start on the Niger with an independent mission-Church, we find, in the history of the other two missionary churches, the view, so popular in earlier missionary theory, that 'mission' and 'young Church' exist in inverse proportion to one another : the Church must grow, the mission must decrease. Both missions were convinced that they were gradually approaching a day when the young churches, the fruits of their work, could be declared independent, so that the Mission could either retire completely or take up an 'ancillary position'. The only difference was the moment envisaged for this 'X-day'.

This partly explains the fact that, for the Korean Church, this day did not have the same dramatic meaning that it had for the Batak Church, whose whole history, through child-like trust, tolerance, resignation, opposition, urge to liberty, ultimate triumph, was characterized by the expectation that the day would surely come. This 'X-day' played a similarly significant part in the history of the Batak Church as in other mission-churches. That Church spent far too much energy in its determined struggle for a constitution, so very similar to the contemporary political struggle, instead of using its strength in the proper work of the Church. This constitution was expected to free the Church from the Mission's tutelage, and doubtless, the expenditure of effort referred to was justified by the Church on those grounds.

The contrast between the Batak and the Korean Churches proves that 'X-day' is a mere fiction. Whereas in the latter, the question of devolution arose after only twenty-two years, the former did not achieve complete autonomy even after seventy years. And yet both young churches, as well as the Nigerian Church, continued to need the help of the older churches and to ask for it. In the case of the Batak Church, as well as many other mission churches, it was not the parent Mission which determined 'X-day', but political events in the outside world, without respect to the actual degree of maturity achieved by the young Church.

It sounds like a piece of unintentional irony that a director of a Lutheran Missionary Society could declare, with reference to this development :

> 'In other mission fields the world wars have led to the formation of young Churches; with us in South Africa the world wars have not had this effect.'

Such a statement proves Visser 't Hooft only too right when he says :

> 'The much quoted Rediscovery of the Church has not yet had a full and lasting effect on the life of our Churches. There is still a great deal of secular thinking with regard to the church.'

According to the Bible, wars have not the power to form churches. What actually happened was that the political events isolated the young churches from the ecumenical fellowship, and they regarded this as liberation, misled by the false conception of autonomy instilled by the Western Mission. One positive result was that some missionaries' consciences, rudely awakened by these events, realized anew that 'a congregation comes into being through preaching about Jesus Christ and through baptism'.

That erroneous theory of autonomy had its theological ground in the limitation of the missionary task to pioneer work, and its historical cause in the fact that the Western Protestant churches had to begin with no missions. In the West, missions were a separate enterprise of particular groups within the Church, the 'missionary-minded' as they are still sometimes called. This could not lead to anything other than the formation of non-missionary churches on the mission-field. It was not Anderson and Allen who set their stamp on the international conception of 'Mission', but Venn and Warneck. Even Karl Hartenstein in 1929 still refers to Missions and Churches as two separate things in the life of the Kingdom.

Not until Willingen did the new understanding win through, that the call to Mission is the decisive reason for the earthly existence of the Church. Representatives of the younger churches stated :

> 'We should cease to speak of Missions and Churches and avoid this dichotomy not only in our thinking but also in our actions. We should now speak of the Mission of the Church.'

Instead of being an occasional enterprise on the part of particularly interested or enthusiastic persons, Mission is here raised to the status of a permanent function or 'mark' of the Church. That is why each group of Christians shares in the responsibility for proclaiming the reign of the King as far as the ends of the earth.

This, however, means that there is no longer any relation of 'inverse proportion' between Church and Mission. At Willingen, Dr. D. G. Moses of India denied the validity of Venn's and Anderson's formula.

> 'The accepted definition of an independent Church which had all too often been confused with the definition of an indigenous Church, is a "self-supporting, self-governing and self-propagating community". The circumstances of the present intensify what is inherent in the nature and growth of the Church, namely the necessity for the acceptance of responsibility which found expression in this historic formula. But if self-sufficiency and autonomy are isolated as ends in themselves they lead to a dangerous narrowness of view. They have meaning only as expressions of the Church's worshipping and witnessing character. We need to apply tests deeper in content and wider in scope.'

The ultimate aim of missions is no longer the organizational independence of the young Church : it is rather the building up of a Church which has itself a missionary out-reach. Hartenstein gladly acknowledged this by writing in 1952, the year of the Willingen Meeting :

> 'Seen from the New Testament, mission is the task given by the Lord Jesus Christ to His Church, to proclaim His Gospel of the Kingdom in all the world. It is the Mission's duty to see that the Gospel is constantly proclaimed.'

Seen from this aspect, the imaginary X-day ceases to obscure the relation between Mission and young Church.

In the missionary history of a country the young Church finds a relation, not only to the missionaries who serve it, but also to the Church which sends the missionaries and which appears to the young Church as the parent Church. We saw earlier that, for the sake of the continuation of mission, this relation must not be simply broken off as soon as the young Church has achieved a constitution. The development of the Batak and Korean Churches in their temporary isolation, mentioned already, proves that this breaking off may cause spiritual harm to the young Church itself.

Another way of expressing what we meant by the responsible selfhood of the Church is in co-operation. This was tried out in Korea but, as we saw, proved impracticable, partly because it resulted in the missionaries' becoming a part of the young Church itself, and partly because it led to a division of tasks which prevented the young Church from realizing its responsibility for certain spheres of church-activity. In other mission-fields, co-operation occasioned constant disputes about competency.

The Whitby watchword 'Partnership in Obedience' did not solve this dilemma. Rather did it increase the obscurity, because it gave the young Church the chance to restrict, and even to obstruct, the obedient 'older Church' in following its own call to Mission. We saw an example of this in the post-war relation between the Indonesian churches and their European parent churches.

At Willingen the attempt was made to overcome this tension by regarding missionary work from a consistently ecumenical point of view, i.e., by trying to abolish the contrast between older and younger churches in the unity of the Universal Church. But the demand that every group of Christians should be responsible for the entire world-mission of the Church is unrealistic, and this ecumenical conception of the Universal Church lacks historical insight.

Many try nowadays to deny that there is any distinction between older and younger churches : there obviously exists a genealogical relation, but generally the two are distinguishable by their different degrees of spiritual development. Indeed, after the war the Batak Church recognized the Rhenish Mission as her parent.

The Mission's work must not only be regarded as pioneer work.

The Mission is called, in the ecumenical life of the Church, to be a herald to the world and to strengthen the young churches which, like some of the older churches, all too often give evidence of spiritual deficiency, 'that which is lacking in your faith' as St. Paul says to the Church at Thessalonica (I Thessalonians 3.10). It is correct to say that a direct missionary appeal to the world was an exception in apostolic times. St. Paul rather used first the framework of the old 'chosen people', and then the Christian local congregations.

In the primitive Church, the apostles bore the responsibility for the young churches. Today, the young churches grow out of the service of the Universal Church, and in each case it is a certain older Church, within its own denomination, which represents the Universal Church to the young Church. In view of the lack of a Universal church-organization, and the denominational separations within the Universal Church, the young Church cannot by-pass her parent Church to effect a direct connexion with the Universal Church. From the theological point of view, the parent Church is the unit which, in the name of the Universal Church, takes responsibility for the growth of a particular young Church. The Universal Church, as a whole, owes this to the young Church, but for practical reasons cannot discharge this duty in ordinary service.

In theory, the total Church has the responsibility, and, in proportion to the degree of unity and co-operation achieved—especially through ecumenical undertakings like the World Council of Churches and world denominational movements like the Lutheran World Federation—the possibilities for organizing ecumenical fraternal service on a broad basis become more numerous. We saw something of this development after the war, in the labours of the International Missionary Council and the Lutheran World Federation, on behalf of the isolated Batak Church. But regular assistance given to the young churches in their particular needs can best be furnished by the parent Church which knows the structure, concerns and personnel of the daughter-Church most intimately, because of their historical connexion. As we showed, this was fully recognized when the Rhenish Mission was asked to collaborate in the ecumenical programme of aid to the Batak.

It is not, therefore, a question of the parent Church's monopoly concerning the daughter Church, or of legal status, but of the task of discharging, in a practical way, the ecumenical responsibility as taught by the New Testament. Although all the apostles were jointly responsible for the whole of early Christendom, St. Paul felt in a special way the 'father' of his mission churches (I Corinthians 4.14-16). This did not prevent St. Peter writing epistles to the mission churches in Asia Minor, and the apostles in general from visiting and temporarily leading local churches which they had not founded.

This ecumenical responsibility in the early Church, however, did not imply any one-sided submission on the part of the mission-churches to the representatives of the mother Church in Jerusalem or elsewhere. The apostolic assistants whom St. Paul chose from among the mission-churches very soon became a staff of new officers for the whole Church, acting as fully recognized ecumenical liaison workers. St. Paul's missionary churches acknowledged in their charitable collections that the original Church in Jerusalem had historic rights, as the parent Church, but they did not acknowledge any primacy of authority on the part of that ancient Church.

In a similar way, the young churches of today very early begin to give help to the Universal Church, and, in particular, to the parent Church. The young Church feels a debt of gratitude to the parent Church and so has a responsibility for it. So the Spirit who flowed from the older Church now begins to flow back to it. Mission reports, and the important liaison service of the missionaries who are temporarily in their home-country, aid this process; but, above all there are the representatives of the young Church itself who more and more frequently do apostolic service to the parent Church on behalf of the daughter Church. In these circumstances, expressions like 'older' and 'younger', parent and daughter, imply no essential primacy or inferiority, but for the most part simply indicate historical facts.

A special feature in these days, and one with which we are becoming increasingly familiar, is the existence of the younger church-leaders who serve the Universal Church in various capacities, visiting the churches of other countries, often attending ecumenical gatherings as well as denominational consultations. These men and women are God's gifts to His whole Church, and are an increasing source of spiritual strength to Christians of all lands and traditions. Thus, the ecumenical inter-change between the parent Church and the daughter Church will become more and more alike, in the same degree as, through church-growth, the 'things that are lacking' in the way of spiritual experience disappear, until finally this inter-change can be put on a broader basis within the framework of the whole denomination.

There is, however, one condition for this necessary enduring connexion between the parent and the daughter Church. The former must be a Church in the true sense. Only a Church, i.e., a communion constituted by Word and Sacrament, can claim to represent the Church Universal. The post-war development, not only in the Batak Church, shows that a genuinely ecumenical communion is hardly possible between a young Church and a missionary society if the latter is merely a voluntary association, and not really the sending branch of a Church. As Allen hinted, it is difficult for a missionary society to fit into an ecumenical union. The society will be tempted in many cases to preserve its status in the mission-field and will be regarded by the nationals as a foreign enterprise. This is often borne out by its claim to property as a society, and by the special organization of its missionaries. In the future, this may have far-reaching consequences for the missionary societies. Unfortunately, we lack space to discuss the difficulties connected with it, for example those arising from the fact that some supra-denominational societies are supported by a number of different denominations.

It is easy to deduce the missionaries' task in the young Church from what has been said already about the relations between the parent and daughter churches. We saw quite plainly, in our second part, that the missionary ought not to occupy permanently appointments belonging to the local structure of the young Church, since these tend to make him, as it were, indispensable, requiring his constant residence in the country. He should neither serve the local Church as its sole responsible minister for the Word and Sacraments, nor permanently occupy a leading administrative position in the supra-congregational organization. If he does so he will impede the younger Church's development towards responsible selfhood, or goad it into opposition, and if he has to leave the country for any reason he will leave the young Church helpless.

The missionary's specific tasks result from the two-fold nature of his vocation : as a 'herald', a witness to the world, and as an ecumenical link between the churches. The Whitby Conference defined the missionary's position as 'an agent of the Church Universal, commissioned by one part of the Church for service in another part'. That means that he will preach to the non-Christians in collaboration with Christian nationals, or, if in certain areas today he is unable to do this, he will instruct and encourage his national colleagues. Other functions of the missionary will include those of teaching and visiting within the Church, fostering the Church's spiritual growth by proclaiming and expounding the Word of God, helping the Church to understand the meaning of Christian discipleship and discipline, especially when the Church tends to err in some aspect of the Christian life, and helping the leaders of the Church to become rooted and grounded in the faith.

The calling of a missionary is really a special version of the supra-local ministry in the Universal Church, on the lines that we have already indicated, as distinct from the institutional administration and activity of the purely local Church. Earlier, we characterized a bishop as the successor of the apostles in their permanent functions. We must treat this episcopal office more specifically now, in-so-far as the bishop is closely connected with the Church of his own country, and can thus exercise the ecumenical functions of the early Christian apostles, prophets and teachers only to a limited extent. This, of course, is one of the consequences of the tragedy of disunity. Here we see one of the most significant aspects of the foreign missionary's position today : he is a living embodiment of the world-wide communion of the Church, and, as such, supplements the local ministry of the bishop or other leader. As the missionary does not claim any administrative or constitutional position in the young Church, at least in his position *qua* missionary, the Church will raise no objection to his collaboration, unless there had already occurred a sad deterioration of relations with the parent Church.

In addition to these main functions, the missionary has to exercise certain special functions such as those emphasized by

Merle Davis as being included in the 'comprehensive approach' of the Mission; for example, medical, educational social and cultural work. These tasks, however, are to be integrally related to the missionary service of preaching and teaching, otherwise they will end in secularization.

The missionary will have to be particularly mindful of the humble devotion enjoined in Matthew 20.25-27 on those engaged in Christ's work, though this will not in any way detract from the authority of his vocation. Christ's example of self-sacrifice did not diminish the authority of His mission but rather exalted it, as St. Paul emphasizes in his great passage in Philippians 2. The missionary is called to be obedient, not to the young Church, but to Christ, or, shall we say, to the young Church only within the context of his obedience to Christ, the common Lord of both the young and the old Church.

The principles of Whitby, according to which the missionary is not to come unless the young Church specially invites him, need re-thinking. The experience in Indonesia after the war shows where this policy can lead. The old Church had good reasons for taking advantage of what it considered its 'right of visitation'. This is our objection to the recent swing of the pendulum in missionary discussions, according to which, the missionary, no longer in any patriarchal or even paternal role in relation to the Church, is to be content to do the work of an ordinary 'hand', with no responsible voice in the direction of the enterprise. We disagree with those who, because of certain unhappy experiences, demand the withdrawal of all foreign missionaries, so that the young churches can decide for themselves whether they want to call in individual Western specialists.

As to the extent to which missionaries from older churches should serve the younger churches, the words of Matthew 9.38 are still valid : 'Pray ye therefore the Lord of the harvest, that He will send forth labourers into His harvest'. There cannot be any excess of missionary service if it really restricts itself to spreading the Word and 'seeketh not its own'. In fact, we hear very little today, in responsible church-circles in Asia and Africa, that suggests in any way that the younger churches not only do not need, but also do not want, the fellowship and service of foreign missionaries who will serve in this spirit, enjoined on His followers by our Lord Himself. The contrary indications of a few years ago were the natural reactions to the older missionary paternalism, from churches in lands throbbing with new national self-respect and vitality. The self-respect and the vitality are still there, but the churches understand, perhaps more clearly than they did a few years ago, that paternalism is not an indispensable and ineradicable mark of missionary service. There are in fact only two limits to the work of missionaries in a young Church: possible government restrictions and the demands of the world-wide deployment of missionary resources.

Finally, the relations between parent Church and daughter Church have to be considered in a fully ecumenical context, especially in these days when, on both sides, there is increasing restlessness over 'our unhappy divisions'. It is probably true to say that this restlessness is more a general characteristic of the whole Church, as distinct from certain leaders, in Asia and Africa than it yet is in the West, and it is imperative that any Western Church concerned about its relations with a daughter Church there should realize that, in its daughter's eyes, some aspects of its alleged maturity may seem dangerously near to decay.

There are two important reasons for discussing the question of church-union here. First, because union means that a constitutional autonomy, characterized by ecclesiastical separation, is given up in favour of a higher union, and, secondly, because it involves at the same time the need to evolve a new statement of the Church's principles of faith, as well as order, to take account of the new situation. This is truly a test of the Church's 'spiritual selfhood'.

We saw during our historical survey that, in the evolution of young churches, union is a central question. As soon as a young Church has reached the stage of self-realization which prompts it to enter with other local churches into a relation of spiritual co-operation, it discovers other types of churches in the same area and in the whole world with which it must achieve a satisfactory relation. It realizes, sooner or later, that organic union is as necessary as it is difficult. The way in which the young Church solves the task of playing a responsible part in the endeavours to bring about such a union is a yard-stick for its maturity in the faith.

The Batak Church's main reason for application to join the

Lutheran World Federation was the need for help, primarily for material help. This has been criticized as an illegitimate and unworthy motive for union. This criticism would be valid if material considerations had been the only ones, and if the resulting measures had violated the young Church's denominational conscience. We have already seen that this was not the case. On principle, however, the objection to 'impure motives' springs from a mistaken spirituality, which overlooks the fact that the New Testament conceives the Church as an organic whole, both body and spirit. In connexion with the collection from the churches on behalf of the parent Church, St. Paul mentions 'the fellowship of the ministering' which unites the Church in all lands.

When the young Church wants to become an organic part of a larger church-unit it shows a healthy realization of the value of this ecclesiastical union in love, which includes material as well as spiritual blessings. The purity of the young Church's motives for union is proved if it is prepared to accept spiritual and not only material help, and is ready to serve the Church as a whole. The crucial test of any church-union is : how far does it induce an active exchange of energy for the benefit of the common triple task of the Church?

When, in 1907, the Korean Church, and, in 1952, the Batak Church, joined denominational world unions, not only were the two young churches themselves interested, but so were the denominational unions. In connexion with the Batak Church's joining the Lutheran World Federation there were, it is true, those who stigmatized as 'denominational imperialism' the denomination's desire to grow and increase its sphere of activity. This attitude is justifiable, however, only if the emphasis on one's own denominational tradition is to be regarded as in itself sinful, or if the relation between the young Church and the denomination is not a genuine relation of Christian brotherhood. There is no sufficient ground for such a doubt in the case of these two particular young churches. Apart from this denominational problem, the urge to grow, shown by the denominational world communion, must be recognized as a genuine concern on the part of a branch of Christ's Church. The whole denomination is here showing a desire to undertake responsibility for all its members throughout the world, to establish spiritual contact between them, and thus to protect them from the temptation to isolate themselves. That was the decisive reason why the various Anglican dioceses formed the Anglican Province of West Africa. A constitutional independence of individual units of the Church can be justified only for external, practical reasons; it remains relative and must always be counter-balanced by the various church-units serving each other and welcoming each other in Christian love.

The essential unity of the Universal Church necessitates visible, organic union, which, at the present stage of ecumenical development, can often be achieved only through the denominational world federations. Although, within these federations, the ecumenical relation between parent and daughter churches is particularly close, the parent Church itself does not bear all the responsibility for the younger Church but carries out this duty in the name of the whole communion, in which all the members are called to serve each other. Therefore, the permanent service of the missionary sent by the parent Church is supplemented by visits from representatives of other member-churches of the communion, serving to confirm, or even, in certain circumstances to restore, the unity of the Church. A young Church which, standing on its rights as an autonomous congregation, refuses to accept this service, threatens the unity of the Body of Christ which includes this 'right of visitation' on the part of all the members.

The ecumenical movement has always received its strongest impulses from the missionary movement and the young churches. It is, as John Mackay declares, 'a child of the Mission'. The reason was that the young churches, surrounded on all sides by overwhelming non-Christian majorities, regarded it as a shameful and unwarrantable cause of offence to display to their countries a Church 'by schisms rent asunder'. We need hardly be reminded of Bishop Azariah's famous words at Lausanne :

'Unity may be theoretically a desirable ideal in Europe and America, but it is vital to the life of the Church on the mission field. The divisions of Christendom may be a source of weakness in Christian countries, but in non-Christian lands they are a sin and a scandal.'

The interdenominational efforts towards union in Nigeria,

Indonesia and Korea were inspired by this idea, although they have not so far been successful. In Protestant Missions the missionary call is more and more emphasized as the decisive factor which renders church-union necessary : its advocates point to John 17.21-23 and to the young Church's almost universal desire, even demand, for union. Exegetical study, however, reveals that the meaning of the texts just referred to is that the unity of the churches is genuine only if it is founded on the one faith in Christ as the Head of the Church.

As the Indonesian example showed, the young Church's desire for union need not always have a missionary objective : it may spring from a feeling of national solidarity. The young churches think they have to prove to the Government their right to exist, by breaking off any ecclesiastical connexions with the churches in the West, and by forming a single independent national Church. Thus there are strong reservations against regarding outside pressure as a valid reason for the Church's efforts to unite. Its importance for church-union is similar to that of nationalism for church-autonomy : it is a warning from outside which demands attention, but it has no constitutive power of itself.

Efforts at Church union are genuine only if they spring from the one faith in the one Lord and aim at obedience to the missionary call. If the missionary connexion with the parent Church is preserved, this can be taken as evidence that the motive was spiritual and did not spring simply from the Church's nationalist consciousness.

When the Batak Church managed to join the Lutheran World Federation; when the attempt at church-union in Korea failed, and when church-union in Nigeria was delayed, the denominational factor was an important one. It manifested itself in a number of ways : the fear that the Batak Church might be hemmed in by denominational barriers, and, on the other hand, the fear that the Anglican Church of the Niger and the Presbyterian Church in Korea might lose their denominational character.

In each case we saw that the impulses to denominationalism or to denominational union did not come from the young churches themselves, but from the missionaries, or rather from their parent churches. It is true, the missionaries, by their extensive influence, had taught the churches to feel at home in the parent churches' type of denomination, so that the demand to give up the form of denomination to which they had been accustomed was received by them with reserve. Nevertheless, the three churches themselves were ready to take this step, and if the question of union had been put to them at an earlier stage, or if the parent churches had not tried to force their own tradition upon them, the denominational factor would not itself have prevented the union from coming into being. It is a theological problem whether the relation of the young churches to their parent denominations can be justified, if it, in fact, restricts their legitimate freedom in Christ. We again encounter the problem of doctrinal autonomy, this time in connexion with the liberty of the young Church over against the various confessions of the Western Protestant churches. There are missionary leaders who do not consider that the young churches have achieved what we have called 'responsible selfhood' until they share with conviction the denominational standpoint of their parent churches. One free-Church Lutheran, the Rev. W. Hopf, in recording his views on the autonomy of the Church, asks :

> 'Will the autonomous young Churches in what were formerly Lutheran mission fields really become and remain Churches of pure doctrine—or will the congregations gathered by Lutheran missionaries finally be submerged in the unionism and syncretism of a single world-wide Protestant Church?'

Confessional Lutheranism, in so far as its conception of the Church is based on the traditional Lutheran statement, the *Confessio Augustana,* section vii, finds itself on the horns of a dilemma. This statement means that the smallest local congregation which has the Word and Sacraments is directly connected with Christ : this could be used to justify the most uncompromising form of Congregationalism. Yet, for the sake of purity of doctrine, confessionalists like Lutherans cannot use Congregationalist methods but must use patriarchal and 'educational' forms until their goal, the independent denominational Church, has been reached. Hence, Hopf is forced to state that a selfhood firm enough to hold its own against 'old and new heresy', without missionary help, 'can only be gradually achieved', and this takes us back to Gustav Warneck's position.

We can escape from this dilemma only if we rightly understand the meaning and limits of the celebrated Lutheran statement referred to. This gives us an implicit definition of the Church, but does not say anything about its form. That is, it does not answer the question in Luther's catechism : 'How does that come about?' We must investigate everything the Reformers, or other great teachers of the Church, have had to say on the question of church-order, and further correct and supplement this evidence by the New Testament statements about it. The liberty of even the youngest and smallest branch of the Church can be fully realized only when it is tested and protected by the universal *ecclesia*. Without this permeating influence, liberty might lead to heresy.

Apart from the concern for 'Faith and Order' which is caused by a sense of spiritual responsibility, all efforts at union spring also from a variety of 'non-theological factors' which can be summed up in the human urge to self-assertion. Fundamentally, the organization wants to preserve its own form and its own power, which it is most reluctant to give up. This instinct of self-assertion is to be distinguished from genuine spiritual steadfastness. It does not do everything possible in order to remove obstacles to church-union, and, instead of using spiritual means, like a common confession of faith in the one Lord, resorts to diplomacy and psychological or even economic, pressure. Both parent and daughter Church suffer from this human weakness, as we saw in the ecumenical history of the Nigerian, Batak and Korean Churches.

It is not always easy to unmask these motives as they adopt a very convincing spiritual camouflage. The parent churches are subjectively quite convinced that they have to fight for their cause as for the Church of Christ. There are only two remedies : the courage to face 'denominational euthanasia' and the renunciation by the parent churches of any possessive rights over 'their' Asian or African mission congregations, a renunciation which does not imply abandoning all responsibility. The denominations have to recognize that their purest and most venerable doctrinal confessions, their most beautiful forms of worship, and their most effective church-constitutions, are not identical with the Church itself and can be re-created by the Church.

Conversely, we discovered that, while the three young churches, discussed here, certainly felt the oft-quoted desire for union on the mission-field, at the same time, the human urge to self-assertion was directed not only against any plan for organic union, but even against proposals for co-operation; furthermore, it even led to schisms in the churches themselves. The chief motives were nationalism, local patriotism, group loyalty, leaders' ambition, spiritual rigidity, lack of readiness to forgive. The young churches, too, had a tendency to disguise this instinct of self-assertion by advancing all kinds of theological arguments. These illegitimate motives were really solely or largely responsible for the separations; this was shown by the fact that some schisms could not be healed even when the original causes no longer existed, and the fact that during the schism the motive or rather the justification was altered.

The will to self-assertion as the chief enemy of church-unity makes it apparent that the ecumenical problem is not solely a theological one. No denominational discussions and no statements of church-order can counteract the assertion of illegitimate autonomy : the problem is rather one of Christian ethics. The will to union presupposes brotherly love, self-denial and Christian obedience. A truly ecumenical spirit takes all bitterness out of the denominational problem by 'love for the heretics'.

The ecumenical efforts of the three young churches proved that the 'horizontal' union is easier than the 'vertical' one, i.e., that partners of a similar or of the same denomination find it easier to agree than those of different denominations. There was no friction at all when the Anglican dioceses formed the Province of West Africa, nor when the four Presbyterian mission churches in Korea formed the Korean Presbyterian Church and joined the World's Pan-Presbyterian Alliance. It took only a few years before the Batak Church could join the Lutheran World Federation, although this was a different situation. But here, too, the 'non-theological factors' may hinder considerably.

The basis of a horizontal union is the knowledge in both parties that the other has in full measure what, according to their beliefs, constitutes the nature of the Church. So, in horizontal union, the knowledge of an already existing unity precedes the organic union. This agrees with the Lutheran conception of the Church and of all ecumenical work. The point is 'to start with the actual unity of the Church'. This differs, however, from the 'unity in love and the Spirit' which Allen sees as the basis of all union. It is the unity which springs from the common possession of the same doctrines, for the Church is founded on the apostolic proclamation.

That is why such a union, even of churches of the same denomination, is always ratified by an act of confession of faith in which the partners, separated by historical developments, both affirm their loyalty to their common denominational heritage. In the West, they usually limit themselves to a renewed acknowledgment of the historic confessional statements. In the mission-field, on the other hand, as is shown by the cases of the Batak Church and the Federation of Evangelical Lutheran Churches in India, a union of this kind may lead to the drafting of a new Lutheran Confession for the whole country in which the Church is situated. So far, no genuinely new confessions within other denominations have emerged.

It was impossible for the Korean or the Batak churches to analyse all the historical confessions within the Presbyterian World Alliance or the Lutheran World Federation, much less did they accept them. The Korean Presbyterian Church was given a brief Statement of Doctrine by its missionaries; the Batak Church drew up its own Confession. From the extreme confessionalist point of view, this meant a compromise, but facts proved that the young churches were quite unable to understand and adopt the historical confessional statements of their parent churches in the West, formulated in a different situation and couched in a vocabulary foreign to the Asian Christians.

A Confession has no more meaning than it can exercise in the life of a Church. That is why the young Church is called to make real to itself the confession of the parent Church. Nobody can relieve it of this duty and it requires a great degree of spiritual maturity, because the young Church must come to know, test and translate the confession. Dr. H. Meyer goes a step further and declares:

'He (the non-European Christian) cannot even recognize the priority of our apparently justified wish that he should at least examine the truth of our Confessions before he himself asks the Scriptures for the truth.'

It is of course correct that listening to the Scriptures has priority, but, when forming its own Confession, the young Church does not stand alone. It is not a question of founding a new Church, but of a young Church springing from its parent Church. As Gustav Warneck was the first to stress, the mission Church cannot, in its connexion with the early Church, by-pass the historical development of the Church.

It is a duty not only of the young Church, but also of the parent Church, to make certain that the new and the old historical Confessions agree : for since the young Church acts as a member of a church-tradition which has developed historically, the whole denominational branch of the Church Universal takes part in the act of confession of the faith.

Once the Confession of the parent Church has been given a new, indigenous expression (always supposing that the young Church recognizes the parent Church's orthodoxy), the young Church is theologically conscious. Its unity with the parent Church is now not only an historical fact but has been expressly acknowledged, and the young Church, in the theological sense, has come of age as a member of the Church Universal. When this unity in the faith has been visibly established, the co-operation or comity, which often already exists between the partners, is strengthened until it becomes a spiritual collaboration capable of answering the triple call to the Church. The form it takes in practice—regional Church, Church Federation or Province—follows from the young Church's external circumstances, such as geographical situation, language, etc.

A young Church, which is satisfied only with horizontal union, either denies the rule of Christ over its neighbouring churches of other traditions—which is hardly thinkable if it is linked with them in comity and co-operation—or is guilty of the sin of self-seclusion. But is it possible for the young Church's efforts towards union to anticipate the result of the denominations' meeting on a wider plane, i.e., of the controversy over 'Faith and Order' in the Ecumenical Movement? We do not consider the missionary situation necessarily makes for church-unity, nor do we think that genuine confessional differences between the parent churches easily disappear between the daughter churches.

There are certain dangers inherent in Hartenstein's summing-up of the result of the Whitby Conference : 'Even if denominational divisions are historically justifiable in Europe, it is a question whether all these differences have to appear in the mission field'. At least the word 'all' ought to be heavily underlined. But where, in the New Testament, do we find an historical justification for denominational divisions at all? In John 17 and I Corinthians 3? However, if A equals B, and C equals D, but A does not equal C, B cannot equal D.

If the young Church, because of the missionary situation, decides to unite with its neighbour Church and thus to break the link with the parent Church, without sufficient doctrinal cause, it commits a new sin against the unity of the Church Universal : the young united Church would then become a new denomination, another 'sect', perhaps, in danger of becoming nationalist. 'Divisions of the Church along national lines are the hardest of all to heal' warned William Temple at Jerusalem in 1928. A union of this kind would not be genuine (even if approved by the parent Church) if it were based on doctrinal subtraction and impoverishment.

The special denominational doctrines are not additions to the fundamental articles, but interpretations (or misinterpretations) of them, without which the old ecumenical Confessions would remain revered but obscure formulae. Hence, the young Church, as even Gustav Warneck, a representative of the Prussian Union of Lutherans and Calvinists, discovered, needs more than this : it needs a Protestant Confession which does not ignore the history of doctrine. This is still important in our age, especially in the church's encounter with non-Christian religions, Christian deviations and secularism.

Union, in the mission-field, entails a fearless struggle for the denominational heritage of the various partners, a struggle in which the parent churches take an active part. Ecumenical development has shown that no denomination can claim the monopoly of truth. That is a hopeful aspect of the efforts at union, which ought to adopt the watchword of the Church of South India : 'Not compromise for the sake of peace but comprehension for the sake of truth'. The conditions for ecumenical efforts are uncompromising veracity, obedience to the witness of the Bible, the ability to judge what is essential in the heritage of one's own Church, and humble readiness to be corrected by others.

There is one reason why attempts at union in the mission-field have a better chance of success than in the West. The conditions for unity are more likely to exist where the Church is obedient to its call to 'go and make disciples of all nations', than where it spends its energies for the sake of self-assertion, in maintaining traditional positions which are no longer relevant and sometimes not even genuine. It is not really conducive to the building up of the Body of Christ, however, if the young Church, which has entered into union with other Christian bodies, then breaks off its links with the parent Church. Similarly, the parent Church, which has given its consent to the union on the mission-field, must act consistently with this position in its own ecumenical relations with other churches at home.

This contribution of the mission-churches to the reunion of the divided older churches would show that the spiritual selfhood of the young churches cannot be treated as an isolated 'missionary problem'. It is a profound theological problem, requiring a full understanding of the catholicity of the Church, based on Ephesians 4.15-16 : 'But speaking the truth in love, (we) may grow up into Him in all things, which is the Head, even Christ' : from whom the whole body fitly joined together and compacted by that which every joint supplieth, according to the effectual working in the measure of every part, maketh increase of the body unto the edifying of itself in love'.

CONCLUSION

'WHERE DO we go from here?' was the question asked by a well-known British missionary writer when he had read the original work on which this present volume has been based. It was a good question. The issues we have been discussing are not simply matters of historical, let alone academic, interest. They lie very near to the heart of the present crisis in Missions—and crisis there certainly is. There will always be a Mission of the Church, as long as there is a Church, for without Mission there is no Church, but it would be naïve to imagine that the pattern of modern Protestant Missions is an essential part of the permanent structure of the Church. The 'euthanasia of a Mission', which Henry Venn foretold, has become a reality in our day, in one area after another, and sometimes the process has not been as happy as the term implies. But, happy or not, and whether we like it or not, the situation now exists in which 'foreign Missions' can operate only within the context of, and in the completest co-operation with, a responsible Church.

The fact that we have sometimes been guilty of creating what Stephen Neill has called a 'myth of the Younger Churches' in no way alters this situation. What is myth today is reality tomorrow, and tomorrow is already here. The Church, like ordinary human beings, becomes responsible by being treated as responsible; responsibility belongs to its nature, the nature it must seek to acquire because it already possesses it. It is a pity if this seems to restrict the freedom of one group of Christians to exercise their missionary vocation among another group of Christians, but it is nothing peculiar.

We do not entrust the shepherding and instructing of our congregations to anyone who claims to be called of God : 'Beloved, believe not every spirit, but try the spirits whether they are of God : because many false prophets are gone out into the world'

185

(I John 4.1). The Indian charge that too often missionaries are 'not called—only sent' is one which cannot be wholly rebutted, and we dare not give occasion for it to be repeated.

It is doubtless possible to deny that the group of Christians in any particular area, calling themselves a Church, are in fact a true Church, although we should take heed under such circumstances not to be found 'fighting against the Spirit'. What is not possible, is to agree, implicitly or explicitly, that a true Church exists, and then, in the name of missionary vocation or anything else, to act as if it did not exist. And this is equally valid whether 'we' are Western or non-Western Christians, whether we are members of a Mission Board or of a Church Council, whether we are 'professional' or 'non-professional' missionaries, or just ordinary members of worshipping congregations in one country or another. But, as we said in the Introduction, for this to be wholeheartedly accepted, something like a revolution is called for in the missionary education of the churches. What would that revolution mean for us, whatever may be the category to which we belong, in the light of the historical and theological data we have been considering? Where, indeed, do we *go* from here?

Revolution may be called for in the attitudes and policies of Mission Boards. By and large, it is true to say the missionary overseas has long been conscious of the need to relate his own mind and activities to the indigenous Church with which he has associated.

He may well have been made conscious of this through the painful repercussions of a local nationalist movement, with streetboys chanting: 'White man go back!' to him as to any other European or American. He may have had the scarcely less, and at times even more, painful experience of feeling that the local Christian community tolerated rather than welcomed him: tolerated him because, at least, he was no charge on local budgets, and might even have been an income-producer by his ability to earn a Government-grant for the institution in which he worked—as well as being some sort of guarantee for the continuance of mission interest and support. But if he persevered, with faith in God and love for the brethren, he would let none of these things move him: instead of giving way to self-pitying talk of frustration, he would understand the struggle of the growing

Church and sympathize with its aims, however ignorantly expressed. This is his life, and he wishes for no other sort of life. This is a life full of opportunities for showing Christian grace, and with many opportunities for witness and true fellowship.

There are many missionaries today who see God's activity in the revolution which is going on around them in Church as well as State, and who see the 'romance' of modern missionary work as something just as real as that of the earlier pioneering days. If such missionaries carry a share of the administrative responsibility for local churches and institutions, they will find it much more natural to view the work from the point of view of the responsible Church, than from that of 'the fathers' in the far-off land of their origin. The fathers themselves have not been uninfluenced by the developments in what was formerly their mission-field. The developments may be completely in line with their own fundamental principles and frequently declared policy, but these fathers on the Mission Boards are pulled in two directions, far more than is the case with their representatives on 'the field'.

The Mission Boards may well be loving fathers to churches in Asia and Africa, but they are also the mouth-pieces and agents of constituencies in Western Christendom (and not always Western nowadays) which have not had the same intimate relation with the responsible Church overseas. If the Church overseas has entered into organic union with Churches of other denominational traditions and connexions, the position of the Mission Board is even more complicated. However enlightened the Board may be, it knows full well that it cannot exist without the support of its constituency. To say : 'Educate the constituency', is easy enough, but what is required is more than the imparting of up-to-date information.

What is required is, much more, the sharing of an experience, and, before that can be shared, a good deal of penitence is necessary, for wrong attitudes in the past—and, still more, for allowing such attitudes to continue into the present—for possessiveness and paternalism, and, above all, for personal pride and a zeal for God which was not always 'according to knowledge'. The issue is fundamentally a spiritual one, and it must, therefore, colour every aspect of the Mission Board's activity. There must not be one face for 'the foreign field' and another face for the home constituency. There must be complete and unwavering integrity, no matter what the cost involved.

We may assume, we hope, that however ignorant some of the supporters of missions may be, their Mission Boards are not strangers to the present situation; that, indeed, they welcome the phenomenon of a responsible Church as a great work of God in answer to their own prayers and labours. With this attitude towards the responsible Church, the Board will show more and not less interest in it, as it hands over to the Church responsibility for decisions on policy which was its own prerogative at an earlier stage. This does not mean that the Mission Board becomes, for example, just the 'London Office' (or Madras Office)—a recruiting or fund-raising agency for a Church in another part of the world. The Board is a responsible body, no less than the Church. It will not be very helpful to attempt to define areas of responsibility, with 'provincial subjects' and 'reserved subjects', as in the days of the old British *Raj* in India.

Christian responsibility, as we have seen, is primarily towards God, in obedience to Him and in commitment to the work of His Kingdom. Both Mission and Church are called to this responsible obedience : this is no guarantee that they will always think alike, but it does imply that they should seek a common mind as partners in obedience. Two cannot walk together except they be agreed, and agreement is possible only with the completest frankness and trust on both sides. Responsible obedience requires information freely shared by both parties, so that they may know all the facts concerning any particular issue, but still more does it demand the fullest confidence in one another as workers together, who are first and foremost 'workers together with Him'.

Responsible partnership must include the right of each partner to contract out of the association if he feels constrained to do so : that is part of the price of responsibility, though it is not always easy for new nations and new churches to realize that this is so. If the Mission Board feels that—with every consideration of the fact of its obedience to its Lord and its love for a group of Christians overseas—it can no longer regard the overseas group as a Church which shares its own theological convictions, and in any way approximates to its own genuine principles of church-order, it must simply say so. One important Mission Board did this over the founding of the Church of South India. Actions like this may be taken hastily, and with less than Christian charity in this fallen world, but it is of the essence of Christian responsibility that they may also be taken in penitence, obedience and suffering love.

There must be no thoughtless recriminations when such a step is taken in full consciousness of the tragedy of the situation. Short of such a step of complete separation there may be occasions of failure to agree on particular issues. The Mission Board's duty on such occasions depends very much on the particular issue.

It is increasingly the custom nowadays, even though far from universal, for Boards to waive the right they had in former times to scrutinize in detail 'field budgets' and to make decisions on details of administration and organization. The Board is not really treating the Church as responsible if it continues to claim such rights which involve, in these cases, no spiritual principles. The Board has responsibility, before God, however, where matters of theological conviction and spiritual heritage are concerned. In such cases it may be necessary to modify the convictions, which are, in any case, always subject to the judgement of the Holy Spirit, or to dissent from the Church's decision, with all consequential steps. This would be an unhappy situation, in either case, but it would be a responsible situation and as such must be accepted. In fact, it would be only rarely that matters would come to such an *impasse*.

We should not exaggerate the implications of Church and Mission responsibility: God is a God of order and not of confusion, and, when His people contract to live together in mutual love and honour, He gives them grace to fulfil their covenant responsibilities. This is as true in Church-Mission relations as in any other relations of the children of God.

But there are two parties at least to this relation, and, if the Mission Board is called to treat the Church which it planted and nurtured as a truly responsible Church, it is equally necessary for the Church to act like a responsible Church. This would be a truism were it not a principle which is not by any means simple to act upon. Development in responsibility is not always a matter of quiet growth: frequently it is attended by explosions and revolutions. Soberness and facetiousness, maturity and puerility alternate bewilderingly in the adolescent boy or girl, as every parent knows, and young churches show the same ambivalence, demanding responsibility, yet often seeking the security and patronage of the earlier situation of dependence.

There would not be the paternalism so often complained of among missionaries if the churches they serve were more generally ready to dispense with the gifts which they bring. This is not meant as a harsh and uncharitable judgement : the difficulties arise largely from historical causes, and it would not be possible to start completely afresh, with brand new attitudes all round, without some repudiation of responsibilities for work and for individuals which both Church and Mission have long since assumed.

To define, in abstract terms, the nature of a responsible Church is only part of our task, the simplest at that; we have to ask where do we go from *here*? What is the responsible thing for *this* Church, in these particular circumstances, and in the relations which exist as part of its spiritual heritage? The simple answer would be that the responsible Church is one which reaches out, not only after support, protection, instruction or even inspiration, but also in mission and service, in discipleship modelled on its Lord—who came not to be ministered unto but to minister—making its own contribution to the world-wide task of building up the Body of Christ in love. Giving as well as receiving. This does not mean essentially giving money towards the funds of the foreign Mission, welcome as are the gifts of the younger churches when they reach mission headquarters. Nor does it mean essentially the sending of missionaries by the Church in its turn to countries overseas, and especially to the country from which it has traditionally received missionaries.

It is held in some quarters today that there will never be a truly responsible relation between Church and Mission until there is a two-way traffic of missionaries. This is an impressive argument, which one would not want to reject out of hand, but, at the same time, it is necessary to emphasize that what is significant in this suggestion is not the mere sending of the missionaries, let us say from India to Britain, but the genuine missionary motive behind the sending.

There is no justification, either in the Bible or in the history of

Missions, for a Church to send out missionaries in order, for example, to prove that it has become mature and responsible. It may well be that a responsible Church is self-supporting, self-governing and self-propagating, but the Church must seek to acquire these characteristics because they are right in themselves, not in order to demonstrate to parent churches, and to the rest of the world, that it has become responsible. Good works do not save a Church any more than they save a man. As Luther said, the good—or saved—man does good works, so we may say that the genuine, responsible Church does good works.

There is a real danger that 'younger churches' in Asia and Africa may be tempted to think of missions to the West as conferring upon them a sort of hall-mark of maturity, an attitude which, besides being spiritually unhealthy, might well militate against the most effective use of those churches' missionary vocation in the world. This is not to suggest that the West cannot do with Missions from Asia and Africa, but such Missions are needed because of the spiritual weakness of the West and not as status symbols for the younger churches. The danger here referred to is just another example of the unfortunate consequences for the Church of an understanding of 'responsible selfhood' which is essentially secular and not one rooted and grounded in Christian obedience.

There is no need for any Church to give artificial expressions of its responsible selfhood : opportunities abound for the responsible Church in every part of the world, not least in Asia and Africa, to contribute to the building up of the Body of Christ by its help in the relief of human distress, its genuine missionary concern, its theological insights, and its share in ecumenical discussions. The glory of the younger churches—a glory which makes the adjective 'younger' increasingly inappropriate—is that, in these and other ways, not least in their challenge to the historic divisions of Western Christendom, they are making a contribution to the World Church of ever-increasing significance.

It is often observed that one mark of maturity is a decreased readiness to imagine slights. 'Love thinketh no evil'. The responsible Church, in East or West, will not feel slighted when missionaries come to it from other countries, even if they come with mistaken motives. It will receive them as men and women who sincerely believe themselves to have been sent by God and so take them into its bosom with loving care that their sin and naïvety will be purged, their vocation deepened and their effectiveness increased.

This calls, as Canon Warren has recently pointed out, for greatly increased pastoral care of the missionary, especially the young and untried missionary with all his mistakes and bewilderment, on the part of the responsible Church of his adoption. It might be good for the missionary to receive at least some of his preparation in the country where he is to serve, especially that part of his preparation which aims at his orientation to the life of the country; it is essential that the Church to which he goes should accept this responsibility for his pastoral care, even if he is not obviously anxious to receive such care, and if, as far as the Church is concerned, he has been 'sent' rather than 'called'. This is part of the responsibility which every Christian has for every other Christian. 'And when you have come to yourself, you must lend strength to your brethren' (Luke 22.32 *NEB*).

The missionary, in his turn, is under a similar Christian responsibility to receive and to show this Christian love. To receive it—not as effusive geniality, but as a mighty power that discerns the inmost thoughts of the heart and lovingly speaks the truth that, in our human weakness and sin, we would prefer not to hear—requires grace on the part of the missionary, for which his 'missionary training' may or may not have prepared him. This is part of the responsibility laid upon him, and until he has come to his own responsible selfhood he is in no position to appreciate, and still less to question, the responsible selfhood of the Church in which he works.

Many devils will war against his soul, as they will against the responsible selfhood of the Church; for both missionary and Church it will remain true, as it was for the first disciples, that 'this kind goeth not out but by prayer and fasting'. The responsible selfhood of the Church and of the missionary can be realized and strengthened only by being denied, by being purged of every secular characteristic, in reverent obedience and glad and willing commitment, under the Cross.

BIBLIOGRAPHY
(selected)

ROLAND ALLEN : *Missionary Methods: St. Paul's or Ours?* 5th Edn. London 1960.
The Spontaneous Expansion of the Church. 4th Edn. London 1960.
(ed. D. M. Paton) *The Ministry of the Spirit.* London 1960.
(with T. Cochrane) *Missionary Survey as an Aid to Intelligent Co-operation in Foreign Missions.* London 1920.

RUFUS ANDERSON : *Outlines of Missionary Policy.* 1856.
(Report of Select Committee)
The Hawaiian Islands: Their Progress and Condition under Missionary Labours. 1865.
Foreign Missions. Their Relations and Claims. Boston 1875.

V. S. AZARIAH : *Christian Giving.* London 1945.

A. M. CHIRGWIN : *The Relationship of the Older and Younger Churches.* London, *World Dominion* 1945.

C. A. CLARK : *First Fruits in Korea.* New York 1921.
The Korean Church and the Nevius Methods. New York 1930.

S. J. W. CLARK : *The Indigenous Church.* London 1929, 3rd Edn.

J. M. DAVIS : *The Batak Church.* Tambaram Report Vol. V.
The Economic Basis of the Church. Tambaram Report Vol V.
New Buildings on Old Foundations. New York 1947.

JOHANNES DÜRR : *Sendende und werdende Kirche in der Missions-Theologie Gustav Warnecks.* Basel 1946.

PETER BEYERHAUS : *Die Selbständigkeit der jungen Kirchen als missionarisches Problem.* Wuppertal-Barmen 1956.

WALTER FREYTAG : *Spiritual Revolution in the East.* London 1940.

NORMAN GOODALL : *Missions under the Cross.* (Willingen papers) London 1953.

C. P. GROVES : *Planting of Christianity in Africa.* Vols. II and III. London 1954-5.

B. GUTMANN : *Gemeindeaufbau aus dem Evangelium.* Leipzig 1925.

F. E. HAMILTON & THOS. COCHRANE : *Basic Principles in Educational and Medical Work.* London 1928.

F. E. HAMILTON & R. ALLEN : *The Nevius Method in Korea.* Reprinted from *World Dominion* 1931.

KARL HARTENSTEIN : *Die Mission als Theologisches Problem.* Stuttgart 1952.

MICHAEL HOLLIS : *Paternalism and the Church.* London 1962.

C. H. KEYSSER : *Missionary Work among Primitive Peoples in New Guinea.* (*International Review of Missions* 1924).

W. KNIGHT : *Memoir of the Rev. H. Venn.* London 1850.

H. KRAEMER : *From Mission Field to Independent Church.* London 1958.

H. C. LAMOTT : *Revolution in Missions.* New York 1954.

K. S. LATOURETTE & W. HOGG : *Tomorrow is Here.* (Whitby Report) 1948.

BLAISE LEVAI : *Revolution in Missions.* Madras 1956.

D. A. McGAVRAN : *Bridges of God.* London 1955.

O. MANNONI : *Prospero and Caliban.* London 1956.

STEPHEN NEILL : *The Unfinished Task.* London 1958.
Creative Tension. London 1960.

R. J. L. NEVIUS : *Methods of Mission Work.* London 1898.

D. T. NILES : *Upon the Earth.* London 1962.

R. K. ORCHARD : *Out of Every Nation.* London 1959.

J. S. PAGE : *The Black Bishop* (S. A. Crowther). London 1910.

H. A. RHODES : *History of the Korea Mission.* Seoul 1934.

J. RICHTER : *Evangelische Missionskunde.* Berlin 1920.
Allgemeine Evangelische Missionsgeschichte.
Bd. I. India. Gütersloh 1924. 2nd Edn.
Bd. V/I. Netherlands E. Indies 1931.

EUGENE STOCK : *History of the Church Missionary Society.* Vol. I-IV. London 1899-1916.

BENGT SUNDKLER : *Bantu Prophets in South Africa.* London 1948.
Church of South India. London 1954.

HENRY VENN : *Retrospect and Prospect of the Operations of the Church Missionary Society.* London 1865.

J. W. C. WAND : (ed.) *The Anglican Communion*. London 1948.

W. A. VISSER 'T HOOFT : *The Renewal of the Church*. London 1956.

MARCUS WARD : *The Pilgrim Church*. (Church of South India).

GUSTAV WARNECK : *Evangelische Missionslehre*. Gotha. 1897-1903.

JOHANNES WARNECK : *The Growth of the Church among the Batak*.

   (International Review of Missions) 1912.

   L. I. Nommensen. Ein Lebensbild. Barmen 1919.

   Sechig Jahre Batakmission. Berlin 1925.

   Living Forces of the Gospel. Michigan 1954.

M. A. C. WARREN : *Partnership*. London 1956.

INDEX